POWWOW Calendar 2001

MW00714680

POWWOW
Calendar 2001

Directory of Native American Gatherings in the U.S.A. & Canada

Native Voices
Book Publishing Company
Summertown, Tennessee

Native Voices ☞
BOOK PUBLISHING COMPANY
PO Box 99
Summertown, TN 38483 USA

1-888-260-8458

ISSN 1059-4965
ISBN 1-57067-111-7

About the Artist:
Red Hawk Woman (Violet Perreault) is a member of the Wet'suwet'en Clan/Moricetown Band, near Smithers, British Columbia, Canada. She is well-known for her paintings of Native dancers and subtle messages of oneness with nature. Her work has opened the hearts of many art enthusiasts and has appeared in various venues in Saskatchewan. Violet spent most of her childhood in foster care and endured many hardships. Her art, which has been a large part of her life since she was a teenager, has given her a strong sense of self. The values of her people has been learned through powwows, dancing, and other cultural events.

 # CONTENTS

All information was verified as correct at the time of printing. However, **changes do occur** so we urge you to **call ahead** before traveling.

POWWOW CALENDAR is not responsible for event changes or cancellations.

The announcement of an event in the calendar is not an endorsement by either Native Voices or Book Publishing Company.

Receive FREE PUBLICITY for your events and help us to expand *POWWOW CALENDAR*. Send us the information on your upcoming 2002 powwows, rodeos, festivals, art shows, and other Native American gatherings for inclusion in *POWWOW CALENDAR 2002*. There is no fee for these listings, but they must be received prior to September 1, 2001, for inclusion in the 2002 edition.

Please send your information to:

POWWOW CALENDAR c/o
Native Voices
PO Box 99
Summertown, TN 38483

pwcal@yahoo.com

POWWOW ETIQUETTE
Liz De Roche

Everyone is welcome to attend a Powwow. It is a wonderful way to learn more about Native American culture. For those of you heading off to your first Powwow here are some basic guidelines to make it more enjoyable.

• Drugs and alcohol are not allowed at Powwows.

• Remember you are a guest at the Powwow and should conduct yourself as such. Be respectful of the traditions and customs. If you are a dancer, honor the protocol of the host group.

• Listen to the Master of Ceremonies for instructions. He will make announcements about special ceremonies, who is to dance and when and where spectators may participate.

• The arbor/dance area is blessed prior to the Powwow and is considered sacred ground. It should be treated with respect. Do not walk across it to get to the other side. If you are dancing use the designated entrances and exits. Treat this area as you would treat a church.

• Stand for the Grand Entry, Flag Song, Veterans' Song, Men's Traditional Dancing, and when requested by the Master of Ceremonies. Men should remove their hats unless they have an Eagle feather on them.

• Cameras, video equipment, and other recording devices should not be used without the express permission of the event coordinator or Master of Ceremonies.

- Certain dances and ceremonies are not to be recorded or photographed. Listen to the Master of Ceremonies who will announce when such activities are to be suspended.

- Consider the privacy of the individual, and ask permission before you record them on film or tape. This includes spectators and craftsmen as well as dancers and singers.

- The first row of benches and chairs placed around the dance area is reserved for dancers and their families. Do not sit on them. Dancers wishing to reserve a space should place a blanket in that space before the dance begins. Please do not sit on someone else's blanket unless invited.

- Do not touch dancers or their regalia. A dancer's regalia is very special to them. Parts of it may be very fragile and easily damaged. Children are often fascinated with the feathers, fur, etc. and may inadvertently cause damage. Please advise them to look with their eyes and not their hands.

- Bring your own chairs to sit on. Ask before you sit down behind a group or dancers to be sure the space isn't being saved for their family and friends. Do not block the view of those behind you.

- Keep your children under control. Don't allow them to play around the dance area.

- Powwow committees are not responsible for accidents, theft, or short-funded travelers.

 # ETIQUETTE

- Many craftspeople are not set up to take bankcards or checks. Plan to have cash for your purchases. Long hours are put into the arts and crafts sold at Powwows. Don't demean the craftspeople or yourself by trying to barter with them. Please use care when handling merchandise, and please watch your children.

- Allow Elders priority in all things.

- Singers and dancers travel long distances to attend Powwows. Blanket Dances are held to help them offset their travel costs. Donate to these dances to show your appreciations. It is all right to enter the arena to donate.

- Respect Mother Earth. Don't drop your trash on the ground. Use the trash cans.

- Give priority to dancers, drummers, and elders in line at restrooms, food stands, etc.

- Be prepared for primitive facilities. Bring water, sunscreen, and toilet paper for your own comfort.

- Everyone is welcome to participate in most social dances, such as the two-step and inter-tribals.

POWWOW TODAY
Liz De Roche

The contemporary Powwow is a link to the past that helps maintain Native Heritage. Seen by outsiders as entertainment due to the singing, dancing, and colorful regalia, the Powwow is a spiritual legacy which should be treated with respect and honor. It is a time for Indian families to be together with other family members and friends. It is a time of sharing, of laughter and tears, of learning, and of caring. It is a time when Indians reflect on their traditions. It is a time to honor the past and celebrate the future.

Indian families travel hundreds of miles to attend Powwows across the continent. Time and distance are not relevant. The renewal of traditions and reinforcement of the heritage is the important thing. It is a time to strengthen the circle.

The word "Powwow" comes from the Algonquin word "Pau Wau" which was used to describe medicine men and spiritual leaders. Early Europeans thought the word referred to the entire event. As Indian tribes learned English, they accepted this definition.

The original dances were held by members of elite warrior societies. They were frequently called Grass Dances and were held for the benefit of tribal members. There were a variety of names used by different tribes for these dances. Among them are Omaha Dance used by the Sioux, Hot Dance used by the Crow, Dakota Dance by the Cree and Wolf Dance from the Shoshone and Arapaho.

The Grass Dance gradually evolved into the Powwow. As Indians began to live on reservations, they had more time to

devote to nonsurvival activities, and dancing became increasingly important. These celebrations were strictly social events until the 1920s when "Contest" dancing became popular. Many local communities still hold social Powwows, but the majority of them now involve contest dancing where dancers compete for prizes.

Contests are judged by dance styles and age group. The dancers are judged on their regalia as well as their dancing ability. Dancing out of beat, losing regalia, and failing to stop on the last drum beat can disqualify a dancer.

A typical Powwow starts on Friday evening with a single Grand Entry and preliminary contest dancing as well as Intertribal dancing. Saturday has two Grand Entries, one in the afternoon and the other in the evening after a dinner break. Sunday usually has a single Grand Entry in the afternoon after which the final competitions are held for the contest.

Many of the larger summer Powwows have a "Camp Day" on the day prior to the beginning of the Powwow. This is a day set aside for visiting and for holding Memorials and Giveaways.

The dance arena, also called an Arbor, may be inside or out. It is blessed before the Powwow begins and is considered to be sacred ground for the duration of the celebration. There should be no drugs, alcohol, profanity, or boisterous behavior in this area. It should be treated like the inside of a church. Frequently there are bleachers for spectators to sit on or people bring lawn chairs.

The front seats of the Arbor are for dancers, singers, and their families. Elders are also given preferred places to sit.

Master of Ceremonies

The Master of Ceremonies keeps the Powwow running smoothly. He is the one who announces the contests, which drums are to sing and explains ceremonies as they take place. Spectators should listen to him to understand what is taking place and to know when cameras and other recording devices are not to be used. The M.C.'s task is not all serious business though and he weaves humorous anecdotes and jokes around his official announcements.

Arena Director

The Arena Director is another important person at the Powwow. It is his responsibility to make sure the dancers and singers have the amenities they need and to organize the Grand Entry. One of his most important duties is to protect a feather if it drops and to assure the proper pick up ceremony for it.

Head Dancers

The Head Dancers are selected by their reputations as dancers and by their knowledge of their traditions and customs. They represent their particular style of dancing and serve as models to the rest of the dancers during the Powwow. Being selected as a Head Dancer is an honor. There are usually two, a man and a woman, but some of the larger Powwows also have a boy and a girl Head Dancer in addition to the adults.

Host Drum

The Host Drum is invited to hold that position at a Powwow based on their reputation and knowledge. They must be ready to fill in if there are any gaps in the drum order if another drum isn't ready to sing. Some Powwows only have

one Host Drum while others have a Northern Host Drum and a Southern Host Drum. There may even be a Canadian Host Drum.

Grand Entry

Each dance session begins with a Grand Entry, a procession of dancers. The Flag Bearers lead the procession carrying the Eagle Staff, American Flag, Canadian Flag, and frequently, the MIA-POW Flag. Being a Flag Bearer is an honor usually given to a veteran, a respected traditional dancer or a traditional elder. Indian Royalty are next, consisting of tribal and organizational princesses and other dignitaries. The Head Dancers lead a single file procession of dancers arranged by category and age. Everyone is asked to stand during the Grand Entry and men should remove their head coverings unless it has an eagle feather.

After all the dancers are in the Arbor, a flag song is sung to honor the Eagle Staff and the flags. Then a respected person, usually an elder, offers a prayer. This is followed by a victory song during which the Eagle Staff and flags are placed in their standards. At this time the Master of Ceremonies will introduce the Head Dancers and Royalty.

Contest Dancing

Contest dancing is divided into categories by age and style. The number of categories varies among regions according to local traditions and to the number of dancers.

The age categories begin with Tiny Tots which are children five years old and under, boys and girls ages 6 to 11 are next, then boys and girls ages 12 to 17. The adult categories are divided between men and women ages 18 to 49. The Golden Age category is for men and women over 50.

The men's and boys' contests are held for Fancy Dancing, Grass Dancing and Traditional Dancing which can be divided into Northern Style and Straight Dancing.

The women and girls compete in Fancy or Shawl Dancing, Jingle Dress and Traditional Dancing. The Traditional Dancing can also be further divided into Northern and Southern Styles as well as Buckskin and Cloth Dresses.

The men's Fancy Dance originated in Oklahoma. These dancers are noted for their fast footwork, athletic ability, and originality. The large double bustles of brilliant colored feathers distinguish these dancers from other types. Their regalia includes angora anklets with sheep bells fastened above them, ribbon shirt, beaded yoke, belt, arm bands, cuffs, and headband. These dancers also wear a porcupine roach on their heads which has one or two feathers attached to them in a spinner.

Grass Dancers

Grass Dancers wear yokes, breech cloths, and anklets covered with strands of brightly colored yarn. On their heads they wear either a bandanna or a porcupine roach. The Grass Dance is noted for its fluid movements and sliding steps.

Traditional Northern Style Dance

The Traditional Northern Style dance represents a warrior scouting before a battle. Their regalia includes a single bustle, usually of eagle feathers, a porcupine roach with a single eagle feather, ribbon shirt, bone hair pipe choker and breastplate, breech cloth, leggings, short angora anklets with sheep bells above them, beaded cuffs, belt, arm bands, and moccasins. The dancer carries a dance staff and a fan usually made from the wing of an eagle. Everyone should

stand during this dance, and men should remove their head coverings (unless it has an eagle feather) out of respect to the dancers and the eagle feathers they wear.

Straight Dancer

The Southern Style or Straight Dancer is easily distinguished by the otter skin trailer decorated with mirrors, beadwork, or ribbonwork which hangs down the back. These dancers also wear long sleeved shirts, breech cloth, and leggings that are trimmed with ribbonwork. Bone hair pipe and bead bandoliers, finger-woven yarn garters and slide tabs, a choker of German silver or beads, a wide loomed beaded belt, and a porcupine roach with a single eagle feather plus an eagle feather fan complete the Straight Dancer's regalia.

Shawl Dance

Women's Fancy or Shawl Dancers wear dresses made of a light weight shiny fabric like taffeta. Their leggings are made from the same fabric or from buckskin. Beaded belt, barrettes, and hair ties finish the apparel. Most important is the shawl which is worn over the shoulders and held out as the dancer steps and twirls. The legend behind the Shawl Dance is of a butterfly who lost her mate in battle. Grieving, she went into her cocoon (shawl) and traveled the world over stepping on each stone until she found beauty in one and was able to begin her life anew. The Shawl Dance is noted for its fancy footwork and fluid movements.

Jingle Dance

The Jingle Dance comes from the Ojibwa Nation. It was popular from 1920 to 1950 and is currently experiencing a strong revival across the nation. The Jingle Dress is made from a fabric such as cotton or taffeta and has numerous "jingles"

attached to it. These jingles are made from snuff can lids. The distinctive sound they make represents waves of water or thunder and is good luck because it scares away the evil spirits. Moccasins, leggings, beaded or concho belts, neck scarf, bag, and an eagle tail or wing fan completes the regalia. Jingle Dancers are judged on their grace and traditional footwork.

Women's Traditional Dance

There are two types of Women's Traditional Dresses: buckskin and cloth. Buckskin dresses are usually heavily beaded across the yoke and have long fringe on the sleeves and along the bottom. This fringe represents a waterfall, continuously flowing, giving life, and persevering like an Indian Mother. The cloth dresses are made from trade cloth and have elk teeth, cowrie shells, dentalium shells, or coins sewn in rows across the yoke. Both of these dresses are enhanced with 15 beaded moccasins, leggings, beaded belt or concho belt, beaded hair barrettes, hair ties, and otter skin hair wraps. The Traditional Woman dancer carries a beaded bag, an eagle feather fan, and a shawl folded over her arm. There are two types of Women's Traditional Dance. One, sometimes referred to as Southern Style, is danced clockwise around the Arbor. The other, Northern Style, is danced in one spot.

Gourd Dance

At many Powwows the Southern Plains tradition of the Gourd Dance is observed. This is a ceremonial dance done only by members of certain warrior societies or clans. Songs are always sung in sets of four, and the group participates in each song four times. Women who are auxiliary members dance behind the men in an outer circle. While the public is

THE POWWOW

welcome to observe these proceedings, absolutely no photos or recordings of any kind are to be made.

Round Dance

A Round Dance is a social dance that all dancers and spectators may participate in. It is done in a clockwise circle stepping to the left in time to the drum beat. Sometimes this is done as a Friendship Dance with two concentric circles moving in opposite directions with people shaking hands as they pass each other.

Blanket Dance

A Blanket Dance is done for a specific purpose such as defraying travel expenses of a special performance group. Several of the Royalty dance around the edge of the Arbor with a blanket outstretched between them to collect monetary contributions.

The Forty-Nine

The Forty-Nine is an impromptu gathering after the powwow events are through for the evening. People gather together to sing "49" songs which are a combination of Native and English lyrics. The lyrics are usually composed by a lover addressing them toward their partner and often have a humorous message tucked into the lyrics. The origin of the name "Forty-Nine" is unclear.

One story is that the laments are sung because 50 warriors went to battle and only 49 returned. Another version, from Oklahoma, is that only 49 dancers showed up at a powwow.

An Intertribal

An Intertribal is a non-contest song that all dancers may participate in. Everyone is welcome to dance, but women should wear dance shawls if not in regalia.

JANUARY

DEC 29-JAN 1
Toppenish Creek New Years Celebration
Toppenish Creek Longhouse
White Swan WA
509 865 5121 ext. 408
509 865 7570 fax

DEC 30-JAN 1
In the Spirit of the New Year
Community Center
Naytahwaush MN
218 846 9749 days
218 573 2190

DEC 31-JAN 1
Leech Lake New Years Powwow
Old Cass Lake High School
Leech Lake MN
218 335 8289

DEC 31-JAN 1
Mid-Winter Powwow
New Town ND
701 759 3469
701 627 3642

DEC 31-JAN 3
Lodge Grass New Years Celebration
Lodge Grass MT
406 638 2601

JAN Date TBA
Midwinter Powwow
Greater Lowell Indian Cultural
Association (GLICA)
Bedford VA Hospital
Bedford MA
978 667 6498 Donna

JAN 1
Turtle Dance
Taos Pueblo NM
800 766 4405

JAN 6
King's Day Celebration: Buffalo, Deer,
Eagle & Elk Dances
At most Pueblos NM
800 766 4405

JAN 7
UNACC Annual Winter Gathering and
Potluck
Fort Devens
Ayer MA
978 772 1306

JANUARY

Sun	Mn	Tue	We	Thr	Fri	Sat
1	2	3	4	5	6	
7	8	9	10	11	12	13
14	15	16	17	18	19	20
21	22	23	24	25	26	27
28	29	30	31			

JAN 12-14
Festival of the Buffalo Powwow
International Market World
1052 Hwy 92 W
Auburndale FL
863 665 0062
www.intlmarketworld.com

Second Saturday in JAN
Muckleshoot Monthly Powwow
Muckleshoot Tribal School
Auburn WA
253 939 3311 ext 153 Walter Pacheco
253 833 6177 fax

JAN 13
First Light Drum: Social & Fundraiser
Moose Lodge
Bennington VT
718 726 2684

JAN 13
Waddell Trunk Show & Benefit Sale
Arizona State Museum
University of Arizona @ Tuscon
Tuscon AZ 85721-0026
520 626 8381
520 626 2976 fax
www.statemuseum.arizona.edu

JAN 13
Morning Star Celebration
Benefit Dance for St. Labre Indian School
John Carroll School
Belair MD
410 838 8333 ext 14 Gary Scholl
glsjcs@yahoo.com

JAN 19-21
Colorado Indian Market & Southwest
Showcase
Denver Merchandise Market
Denver CO
806 355 1610 Randy Wilkerson
txindmkts@tcac.net
www.indianmarket.net

JAN 19-21
Napi Powwow
Peigan Crow Lodge Arena
Brocket AB Canada
403 627 4224 Quinton Crowshoe
403 627 2564
okinapi@telusplanet.net

Third Saturday in JAN
TIA-PIAH Benefit Dance
St Pius V Catholic Church Gym
Pasadena TX
713 475 0221 Dale Adams
Dadams2010@AOL.com
281 448 8435 Grant Gaumer

JAN 20-21
West Valley Fine Arts Festival
Indian Festival Committee
387 Wigwam Blvd
Litchfield Park AZ
623 935 6384 Kala Parker
623 935 7006 Heidi Vasiloff

JAN 22
Evening Firelight Dances
San Ildefonso Pueblo NM
800 766 4405

 # JANUARY

FRAN **WHISPERING BEAR** LUCY

Traditional Supplies

- ANTLERS
- SKULLS
- CLAWS
- HIDES

- TURTLE SHELLS
- TEETH

AND

MORE

5 Dutchess Ave.
Staten Island, N.Y. 10304
Free Brochure

Phone & Fax
(718) 351-6768
www.whisperingbear.com
email: contact@whisperingbear.com

JAN 23
San Ildefonso Pueblo Feast Day
San Ildefonso Pueblo NM
505 843 7270

JAN 27
Thunderbird American Indian
Dancers Powwow
American Indian Community House
404 Lafayette St.
NYC NY
201 587 9633 Louis Mofsie

JAN 27
Portraits in Cloth: Tohono O'Odham
Quilts of Goldie Richmond
Arizona State Museum
University of Arizona @ Tuscon
Tuscon AZ 85721-0026
520 626 8381
520 626 2976 fax
www.statemuseum.arizona.edu

JAN 28-FEB 11
American Indian Exposition
Flamingo Hotel
Stone & Drachman
Tucson AZ
520 622 4900

Pow-Wow Dancer's & Craftworker's Handbook

by Adolf Hungry Wolf

This book is a great resource for dancers, craftworkers, and historians who want to learn more about powwow costumes. **Pow-Wow Dancer's & Craftworker's Handbook** is filled with photographs showing powwow and dance costumes that have been worn during the past 100 years, along with written histories and first-hand accounts of powwow activities. Numerous pen and ink drawings illustrate many of the items worn with powwow costumes. They are accompanied by a discussion of how each of the items were made.

$21.95 USA / $29.95 Canada
(for shipping add $3 US or $3.50 Canada)

Book Publishing Company
P.O. Box 99
Summertown, TN 38483
1-800-695-2241

FEBRUARY

JAN 28-FEB 11
American Indian Exposition
Flamingo Hotel
Stone & Drachman
Tucson AZ
520 622 4900

FEB Date TBA
Cherish the Children
Aih Dah Yung (Our Home) Center
St Paul MN
651 227 4184 Gabriel Strong

FEB Date TBA
Annual Mountain Valley Mall Powwow
Mountain Valley NH
603 539 5015 (Vendors by invitation
only)

FEB 2
Candelaria Day Celebration
San Felipe Pueblo NM
800 766 4405

FEB 2-5
Powwow Cruise
Miami to Bahamas
760 369 2232
adcruise@jps.net
www.powwowcruise.com

FEB Every Saturday
Sandy Osawa Film Series
Mashantucket Pequot Museum
Mashantucket Pequot Resevation CT
800 411 9671
www.Mashantucket.com

First or Second Saturday in FEB
New England Native American Institute
(NENAI) Powwow
Burgess Elementary School
Burgess Road
Sturbridge MA
508 886 6073

First Saturday in FEB
Native New Year Celebration
Suquamish Tribal Center
Suquamish WA
360 394 5266 Peg Deam
360 598 6295 fax
pdeam@suquamish.nan.us
www.suquamish.nsn.us

FEBRUARY

Sun	Mn	Tue	We	Thr	Fri	Sat
					1	2	3
4	5	6	7	8	9	10
11	12	13	14	15	16	17
18	19	20	21	22	23	24
25	26	27	28			

 # FEBRUARY

FEB 3-4
Annual Native American Hoop Dance
Championships
Heard Museum
2301 North Central Avenue
Phoenix AZ
602 252 8840

FEB 4-6
Sinte Gleska Founders Day Powwow
Sinte Gleska University
Mission SD
605 747 2263
605 856 2538
605 867 4115 fax

FEB 8-11
Seminole Tribal Festival & Rodeo
Hollywood FL
954 966 6300 ext 1305
seminloetribe.com

FEB 10
Pequot Cordage Bracelet Family
Workshop
Mashantucket Pequot Museum
Mashantucket Pequot Resevation CT
800 411 9671
www.Mashantucket.com

First or Second Saturday in FEB
New England Native American Institute
(NENAI) Powwow
Burgess Elementary School
Burgess Road
Sturbridge MA
508 886 6073

Second Saturday in FEB
Muckleshoot Monthly Powwow
Muckleshoot Tribal School
Auburn WA
253 939 3311 ext 153 Walter Pacheco
253 833 6177 fax

Second Weekend in FEB
Mouz Pamp Memorial Association Mid-
Winter Powwow
U.P. State Fairgrounds
Escanaba MI
906 789 0505
kocbay@up.net

FEB 11
UNACC Annual Winter Social & Potluck
Fort Devens
Ayer MA
978 772 1306

FEB 16
Indian Law Students Powwow
University of Wisconsin-Madison
Madison WI
608 263 5019
608 833 7990

FEB 16-19
O'Odham Tash
Casa Grande AZ
520 836 4723

FEBRUARY

Third Saturday in FEB
TIA-PIAH Benefit Dance
St Pius V Catholic Church Gym
Pasadena TX
713 475 0221 Dale Adams
Dadams2010@AOL.com
281 448 8435 Grant Gaumer
919 286 3366 (day)
919 286 9401 Joe Liles (eve)
liles@ncssm.edu

FEB Every Saturday
Sandy Osawa Film Series
Mashantucket Pequot Museum
Mashantucket Pequot Resevation CT
800 411 9671
www.Mashantucket.com

FEB 17
Oyate Ho Waste Traditional Powwow
DWU Wellness Center
Mitchell SD
605 995 2637 Jerry Lytle

FEB 17
N. C. School of Science & Math
Powwow
1219 Broad St
Durham NC

FEB 17-18
Indian Artists of America Show
Arizona Indian Arts Alliance
Scottsdale Civic Center Mall
Scottsdale AZ
520 398 2226 Don Owen

FEB 17-19
Washington's Birthday Celebration
Toppenish Longhouse
Toppenish WA
509 865 5121 Yakama Tourism
509 865 7570 fax

FEB Weekend Before Presidents' Day
Casa Grande Outdoor Indian Market
Casa Grande AZ
505 538 2471 Rosalie & Bob Baker

FEB 23
Bark Container Workshop
Mashantucket Pequot Museum
Mashantucket Pequot Resevation CT
800 411 9671
www.Mashantucket.com

FEBRUARY

Sun	Mn	Tue	We	Thr	Fri	Sat
				1	2	3
4	5	6	7	8	9	10
11	12	13	14	15	16	17
18	19	20	21	22	23	24
25	26	27	28			

FEB 23-25
Ancient Voices Benefit Powwow
Myakkahatchee River Park
Interstate 75 & Exit 33 (Sumner Blvd)
North Port FL
941 496 9771 Mark Crazydog
941 496 9771 fax (please call first)
SovereignNationsInc@go.com
http://www.sncpc.home.dhs.org

FEB 23-25
Vero Beach Intertribal Powwow
Indian River County Fairgrounds
58th Avenue (near Kiwanis-Hobart Park)
Vero Beach FL
561 567 1579 after 11 AM Dona

Last Saturday in FEB
Chemawa Birthday Powwow
Chemawa Indian School
Salem OR
503 399 5721 ext 260
mreyes@chemawa.bia.edu

Last Saturday FEB
Stanley Purser Powwow
Port Gamble Tribal Center
Little Boston
Port Gamble WA
360 297 2646

FEB Every Saturday
Sandy Osawa Film Series
Mashantucket Pequot Museum
Mashantucket Pequot Resevation CT
800 411 9671
www.Mashantucket.com

FEB 24
Thunderbird American Indian Dancers
Powwow
American Indian Community House
404 Lafayette St.
NY NY
201 587 9633 Louis

FEB 24-25
Southwest Indian Art Fair
Arizona State Museum
University of Arizona @ Tuscon
Tuscon AZ 85721-0026
520 626 8381
520 626 2976 fax
www.statemuseum.arizona.edu

Late FEB
Deer Dances
San Juan Pueblo NM
800 766 4405

 # MARCH

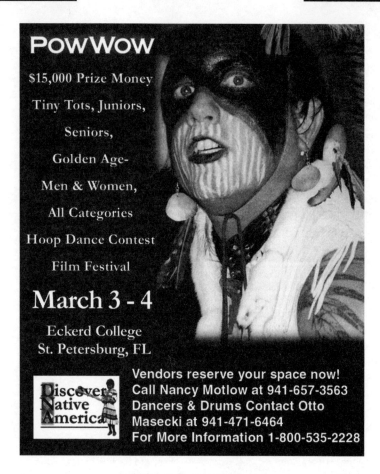

POWWOW

$15,000 Prize Money

Tiny Tots, Juniors,

Seniors,

Golden Age-

Men & Women,

All Categories

Hoop Dance Contest

Film Festival

March 3 - 4

Eckerd College
St. Petersburg, FL

Discover Native America

Vendors reserve your space now!
Call Nancy Motlow at 941-657-3563
Dancers & Drums Contact Otto
Masecki at 941-471-6464
For More Information 1-800-535-2228

MAR Date TBA
Sugar Run Powwow
Dulac Land Trust
Sanbornton NH
603 783 9922

MAR Date TBA
West Texas Native American Association
Contest Powwow
South Plains Fairground
Lubbock TX
806 792 0757 Lew Harmonson

MAR Date TBA
Speelyi Mi Arts & Crafts Fair
Yakama Nation Legends Casino
Toppenish WA
509 865 5121 Yakama Tourism
506 865 7570 fax

MAR or APR Date TBA
Root Feast
Warm Springs Reservation
Warm Springs OR
541 553 3246

MARCH

MAR 1-3
Festival of Native Arts
Fairbanks AK
907 474 7181

MAR 3-4
Discover Native America Powwow
Eckerd College
St Petersburg FL
727 480 9445 Pete Gallagher
727 867 1166 Ross Bannister
941 657 3563 Nancy Motlow (Vendors)
941 471 6464 Otto Masecki (Dancers & Drums)
tribune@semtribe.com
www.seminoletribe.com

MAR 3-4
Heard Museum Guild Indian Fair & Market
The Heard Museum
2301 North Central Avenue
Phoenix AZ
602 252 8840

MAR 3-4
Winter Powwow
State Fair Park
Milwaukee WI
414 774 7119

MAR 4-31
Student Art Show
Five Civilized Tribes Museum
Muskogee OK 74401
918 683 1701 Clara Reekie
918 683 3070
the5tribesmuseum@azalea.net
www.fivetribes.com

MAR 9
Fife Indian Education Powwow
Surprise Middle School
2001 Milton Way
Milton WA
253 922 5949 Patty Butler

Second Saturday MAR
Muckleshoot Mini Powwow
Muckleshoot Tribal School
Auburn WA
253 939 3311 ext 153 Walter Pacheco
253 833 6177 fax

MARCH

Sun	Mn	Tue	We	Thr	Fri	Sat
					1	2	3
4	5	6	7	8	9	10
11	12	13	14	15	16	17
18	19	20	21	22	23	24
25	26	27	28	29	30	31

MAR 10-11
Annual wa:k Powwow
San Xavier Del Bac Mission
Tucson AZ
520 294 5727

MAR 10-11 (Tentative)
Tiospaye Powwow
University of South Dakota Traditional
Powwow
Vermillion SD
605 677 6875 Doyle
dtipeonh@usd.edu

Second Weekend MAR (Tentative)
E-Peh-Tes Powwow
Lapwai ID
208 843 2253

MAR 12
Nde Daa Exhibition Powwow
Mc Allen TX
956 686 6696 Robert Soto
robtsoto@aol.com
956 583 1112 Betty Russell

MAR 16-18
Indian River Native American Festival
Silver Sands Arena
625 Tomoka Farms Road
New Smyrna Beach FL
904 424 0860

MAR 16-18
Apache Gold Casino Powwow
San Carlos AZ
800 272 2438

MAR 16-18
Indian New Year Gathering
NC Indian Cultural Center
Pembroke NC
910 521 4178

MAR 16-18
Denver March Powwow
Denver Coliseum
Denver CO
303 934 8045 Grace Gillette
303 934 8046
committee@denvermarchpowwow.org
www.denvermarchpowwow.org

MARCH

Sun	Mn	Tue	We	Thr	Fri	Sat
					1	2	3
4	5	6	7	8	9	10
11	12	13	14	15	16	17
18	19	20	21	22	23	24
25	26	27	28	29	30	31

MAR 17
Texas Inter-Tribal Indian Organization
March Benefit Powwow
Rex Baxter Bldg   Tri-State Fairgrounds
Amarillo TX
806 358 3277 Billy Turpin, President
806 358 3112 Marie Lewis
806 378 8082 fax

MAR 17
O'Odham Day Celebration
Organ Pipe Cactus
Ajo AZ
520 387 6849

Third Saturday in MAR
TIA-TIHA Benefit Dance
St Pius V Catholic Church
Pasadena TX
713 475 0221 Dale Adams
Dadams2010@aol.com
281 448 8435 Grant Gaumer

Third Saturday in MAR
Potlatch
Fairbanks Native Association
Fairbanks AK
907 452 1648

Third Weekend in MAR
Great Falls Native American Art
Association Exhibit & Sale
Trade & Industry Building—Fairgrounds
Great Falls MT
406 761 6251 Gladys Cantrell
406 791 2212

Third Weekend in MAR
Calling of All Tribes Powwow
Grand Bois Park
Bourg LA
504 879 2373

Third Weekend in MAR
Mother Earth Awakening Powwow
Stewart Indian School Museum
Carson City NV
775 882 692966

MAR 19
St Joseph's Feast Day
Laguna Pueblo (Old Laguna) NM
800 766 4405

MAR 23-24
Harold A Cedartree Memorial Powwow
ELWC Ballroom Brigham Young Univ
Provo UT
801 378 6849
801 378 3065

MAR 23-25
Texas Indian Market
Arlington Convention Center
Arlington TX
806 355 1610 Randy Wilkerson
txindmkts@tcac.net
www.indianmarket.net

MAR 23-25
Florida Indian Hobbyist
Association Powwow
St Lucy Co Fairground (new)
Ft Pierce FL
561 466 7379
fihanews@aol.com

MAR 23-25
Hozhoni Dayz Powwow
Ft Lewis College Gymnasium
1000 Rim Drive
Durango CO
970 247 7221 Kristi Harper
970 247 7686 fax
hozhonidayz@excite.com

MAR 23-26
Yakama Nation All Indian Basketball
Tournament
Wapato WA
509 865 5121 Lehigh John

MAR 24
Thunderbird American Indian Dancers
Auction
American Indian Community House
404 Lafayette St.
New York City NY
201 587 9633 Louis

MAR 24-25
Grand Village of Natchez Indians
Powwow
Jefferson Davis Blvd
Natchez MS
601 442 0200

MAR 24-25
Spring Competition Powwow
Chinook Winds Gaming and Convention
Center
Lincoln City OR
800 922 1399 Craig Whitehead
541 444 2307 fax
craigw@ctsi.nsn.us

MAR 29-30
Moundville Knap-In
Moundville Archaeological Park
Moundville AL
205 371 2234 Angie Jones
205 371 4180 fax
bbomar@bama.ua.edu (Bill Bomar)
moundvilee.ua.edu

MAR 30-31
Edisto Indian Cultural Festival
Exchange Park (Fair Grounds)
Ladson SC
843 871 2126 Pearl Creel
843 871 8048 fax

MARCH

Sun	Mn	Tue	We	Thr	Fri	Sat
					1	2	3
4	5	6	7	8	9	10
11	12	13	14	15	16	17
18	19	20	21	22	23	24
25	26	27	28	29	30	31

MAR 30-31
NAHA Annual Powwow
Dedmon Center, Radford University
Radford VA
540 980 2203

MAR 30-APR 1
Ormond Beach American Indian Festival
Casement Center
Ormond Beach FL
904 756 7900 Jim Sawgrass

MAR 30-APR 1
Native Ways Indian Festival & Powwow
Georgia National Fairgrounds (I-75 exit 42)
Perry GA
229 787 5180 Jerry Laney
229 787 0642 fax
www.nativewayproductions.com

MAR 30-APR 1
Dance for Mother Earth Powwow
Univ Mich Crisler Arena
Ann Arbor MI
734 763 9044
smmartin@umich.edu
www.umich.edu/~powwow/

MAR 30-APR 1
Tifton Intertribal Powwow
Friendly City Park (I-75 exit 63A, west one mile)
Tifton GA
229 787 5180 Jerry Laney (evenings)
229 787 0642 fax
nativeway@mindspring.com
www.NativeWayProductions.com

MAR 31-APR 1
Central Michigan University Powwow
Athletic Complex
Mt Pleasant MI
517 774 2508

NATIVE AMERICAN CRAFTS DIRECTORY

Second Edition
compiled by Diane McAlister

- Fine Art
- Arts and Crafts
- Rugs and Blankets
- Jewelry and Silverwork
- Beads
- Craftmaking Supplies
- Leather Goods and Furs
- Native American Books
- Audio
- Video
- More!

A Guide for Locating
Craft Shops and Craft Suppliers

A great resource for craftmakers, wholesalers and collectors. Over 1,000 entries to help locate hard-to-find Native American products, organizations, and resources. Sources are listed for classic Indian art, traditional handcrafted items, contemporary Southwest-style home decor, wholesale craftmaking supplies, beads, Native American books, tipis, and buffalo robes. Entries include address and phone number and are indexed by state and types of products and services offered.

$9.95 US/$14.95 Canada
(for shipping add $3 US or $3.50 Canada)

Book Publishing Company
P.O. Box 99 Summertown, TN 38483
1-800-695-2241

MAR 30-APR 1
Ormond Beach American Indian Festival
Casement Center
Ormond Beach FL
904 756 7900 Jim Sawgrass

MAR 30-APR 1
Native Ways Indian Festival & Powwow
Georgia National Fairgrounds (I-75 exit 42)
Perry GA
229 787 5180 Jerry Laney
229 787 0642 fax
www.nativewayproductions.com

MAR 30-APR 1
Dance for Mother Earth Powwow
Univ Mich Crisler Arena
Ann Arbor MI
734 763 9044
smmartin@umich.edu
www.umich.edu/~powwow/

MAR 30-APR 1
Tifton Intertribal Powwow
Friendly City Park (I-75 exit 63A, west
one mile)
Tifton GA
229 787 5180 Jerry Laney (evenings)
229 787 0642 fax
nativeway@mindspring.com
www.NativeWayProductions.com

MAR 31-APR 1
Central Michigan University Powwow
Athletic Complex
Mt Pleasant MI
517 774 2508

MAR or APR Date TBA
Root Feast
Warm Springs Reservation
Warm Springs OR
541 553 3246

APR Date TBA
All Nations Pigeon River Powwow
Sevier County Fairgrounds
Sevierville TN
423 378 0192 Leon Gilliam

APR Date TBA
Oyate/AISES Spring Powwow
University of Colorado-Boulder
Solar Hogan Area
Boulder CO 80329
303 492 8874

APR or MAY Date TBA
Powwow
North Seattle Community College
Seattle WA
206 527 3722

APR or MAY Date TBA
Annual Unity Powwow
404 Lafayette, 8th floor
New York City NY
212 598 0100 ext 224

APR 6-7
Making of Relatives Traditional Powwow
Ridgewater College Willmar Campus
Willmar MN
800 722 1151
www.ridgewater.mnscu.edu
NAAG@ridgewater.mnscu.edu

APR 6-7
Native American Awareness Gathering
Ridgewater College Willmar Campus
Willmar MN
320 231 5126 Dennis Waskul
800 722 1151
www.ridgewater.mnscu.edu
waskulde@ridgewater.mnscu.edu

APR 6-8
Native American Arts Festival
Clark County Heritage Museum
Henderson NV
702 455 7955

APR 6-8
Kansas City Indian Market
International Trade Center
Overland Park KS
806 355 1610 Randy Wilkerson
txindmkts@tcac.net
www.indianmarket.net

APR 7
A.I.R.O. Powwow
University of Wisconsin-Stevens Point
Stevens Point WI
715 346 3576 Sharon Cloud
scloud@uwsp.edu

First Weekend in APR
Indian Week
New Mexico State University
Las Cruces NM
505 646 4207 Lydia

First Weekend in APR
Time Out Wacipi
University of North Dakota
Grand Forks ND
701 777 4314

APR 7-8
DeSoto Caverns Park Spring Indian Fest
Childersburg AL
800 933 2283 Joe Beckham
256 378 3678
desoto@mindspring.com
www.cavern.com/desoto

APR 7-8
Western Michigan University
NASO Contest Powwow
WMU University Arena
Kalamazoo MI
616 387 2279
616 387 3160

APRIL

Sun	Mn	Tue	We	Thr	Fri	Sat
1	2	3	4	5	6	7
8	9	10	11	12	13	14
15	16	17	18	19	20	21
22	23	24	25	26	27	28
29	30					

Red Hawk Woman

Violet Perreault

*I*f you were intrigued with the painting *Navajo Boy* on the cover of this calendar, you'll want to see more of **Violet Perreault's** stunning art works. Ten of her exclusive pieces are available in her **Red Hawk Woman's** 2001 calendar, as well as on posters, greeting cards and post cards. **Red Hawk Woman, Violet Perreault's** work can be ordered online, by telephone or by mail order.

To order any product, or to make enquiries about the artist, contact the artist's representative:

**RED HAWK WOMAN'S
FIRST NATIONS ART GALLERY**
c/o: ProWrite Communications
Box 95, Dodsland, Saskatchewan, Canada S0L 0V0
Phone/Fax: (306) 356-4634
email: jmayer@microflash.com
www.saskworld.com/RedHawkWoman

*Red Hawk Woman
Calendars*
Singles
$20.00/ea

*Poster
Prints*
Singles
$30.00/ea

Greeting Cards
Singles
$3.00/ea

Post Cards
Singles
$1.50/ea

Prices for Calendars, Cards, and Prints are in Canadian funds.
All products are available at wholesale prices on larger quantities

APRIL

APR 7-8
Art Under the Oaks Indian Market
Five Civilized Tribes Museum
Muskogee OK 74401
918 683 1701 Clara Reekie
918 683 3070
the5tribesmuseum@azalea.net
www.fivetribes.com

APR 7-30
Art Under the Oaks Show
Five Civilized Tribes Museum
Muskogee OK 74401
918 683 1701 Clara Reekie
918 683 3070
the5tribesmuseum@azalea.net
www.fivetribes.com

APR 13-14
Annual Navajo Community College
Powwow
Navajo Community College
Tsaile AZ
520 724 6741 Walter

APR 13-15
Rattlesnake Festival
Apache Fair Building
Apache OK
580 588 3691 Kenneth Looking Glass

APR 14
Dawnland Center Spring Social &
Powwow
Civic Center
268 Gallison Hill Road
Montpelier VT
802 229 0601

Easter Weekend (APR 14-15)
Easter Weekend Celebration
Most Pueblos NM
800 766 4405

APR 19-21
Indian Arts and Crafts Association Trade
Show
Albuquerque NM
505 265 9149 Darien Cabral
505 474 8924 fax
IACA@IX.NETCOM.COM
www.IACA.com

APR 20-21
Texas Gulf Coast TIA-PIAH Benefit
Dance
Albert V Salas County Park
New Caney TX
713 475 0221 Dale Adams
Dadams2010@AOL.com
281 448 8435 Grant Gaumer

APRIL

Sun	Mn	Tue	We	Thr	Fri	Sat
1	2	3	4	5	6	7
8	9	10	11	12	13	14
15	16	17	18	19	20	21
22	23	24	25	26	27	28
29	30					

APR 20-21
Northwest Coastal Gathering
Ballard High School
Seattle WA
206 285 4425 Cindy James

APR 20-22
Haliwa-Saponi Powwow
Haliwa-Saponi Tribal Grounds
Hollister NC
252 586 4017

APR 21 (Tentative)
Apple Blossom Powwow
Farmington NM
505 599 0321 Native American Programs
505 599 0385 fax

APR 21
Mills College Powwow
Mills College
Oakland CA
510 430 2341 ext 1 Ann Metcalf

APR 21
Northwest College Powwow
Powell WY
307 754 6713 Mary Baumann

APR 21-22
Mankato State University Powwow
Blakeslee Football Field
Mankato MN
507 389 5230 Ben Benson

APR 21-22
California Choctaw Gathering
Bakersfield CA
661 836 8270 Theresa Harrison
oklachahta@igalaxy.net
www.oklachata.org

APR 21-23
Frisco Native American Museum
Intertribal Powwow
Ancestral Grounds
Hatteras Island NC
252 995 4440

APR 22-23 (Tentative)
Apigsigtag Ta Reconciliation Powwow
Native American Cultural Center
University of New Hampshire
Durham NH
603 862 0231

APR 26-28
Talihina Indian Festival
Talihina OK
918 567 2539 Carol James

APR 26-28
Gathering of Nations Powwow
The Pit
University of New Mexico
Albuquerque NM
505 836 2810
www.gatheringofnations.com

APR 27-28
Native American Heritage Days
Moundville Archaeological Park
Moundville AL
205 371 2234 Angie Jones
205 371 4180 fax
bbomar@bama.ua.edu (Bill Bomar)
moundvilee.ua.edu

APRIL

APR 28
Graeme Park Native American Cultural
Festival
859 County Line Road
Horsham PA
215 343 0965
www.phmc.state.pa.us

APR 28
Thunderbird American Indian Dancers
Powwow
American Indian Community House
404 Lafayette St.
NYC NY
201 587 9633 Louis

APR 28
Honoring Education Powwow
University of Wisconsin-Eau Claire
Eau Claire WI
715 836 3367 Marge Hebbring
hebbrima@uwec.edu

Last Saturday in APR
Prairie Festival Powwow
South West State University
Gym
Marshall MN
507 537 6018 Sandy or Don

Last Saturday in APR
South Umpaqua Powwow
South Umpaqua High School
Myrtle Creek OR
541 863 6274 Carol

Last Saturday in APR
Red Heart American Indian Festival
Fair Hill Fairgrounds Rte 273
8 miles north of
Elkton MD
410 885 2800 Linda Coates

Last Weekend in APR
Crow Tribe Juniors Handgame
Tournament
Crow Agency MT
406 638 2601

Last Weekend in APR
KYI-YO Powwow
University of Montana
Missoula MT
406 243 5831

Last Weekend in APR
Spring Powwow
Portland State University
Portland OR
503 725 5671
uishi@mail.pdx.edu

Last Full Weekend in APR
Wildlife Prairie Park Powwow
Peoria IL
309 676 0998

APR 28-29
AIC Spring Powwow
Boone County 4-H Grounds
Lebanon IN
765 482 3315

EST. 1980

Harts Lake
Trading Post

35816 58th Ave. S.
Roy, WA 98580
(360) 458-3477

LEATHER, FURS, RAWHIDE, TEETH,
CLAWS, SHELLS, TAILS, HERBS,
DRESSES, SHIRTS, MOCCASINS,
CAPOTES, LEGGINGS, HEADWEAR.
WE ALSO CUSTOM MAKE ANYTHING
JUST THE WAY YOU NEED IT.
WE WELCOME PHONE CALLS FOR
INDIVIDUAL QUOTES.
TRADE OFFERS WELCOME.
CATALOG ON REQUEST.

ANGELO & AMANDA PLATONI

 # MAY

APR or MAY Date TBA
Powwow
North Seattle Community College
Seattle WA
206 527 3722

MAY Date TBA
Spring Planting Festival-GLICA
Greater Lowell Indian Cultural
Association
Historic Pawtucket Indian Site
Tyngsboro MA
978 667 6498 evenings

MAY Date TBA
Aurora U Powwow
University Museum
Aurora IL
630 844 5402

MAY Date TBA
Rosebud Elder Day Games
Rosebud SD
605 856 2538
605 867 4115 fax

MAY 1
San Felipe Feast Day
San Felipe Pueblo NM
800 766 4405

MAY 3
Santa Cruz Feast Day
Taos Pueblo NM
800 766 4405

MAY 3-6
Mata Ortiz Learning Expedition
Arizona State Museum
University of Arizona @ Tuscon
Tuscon AZ 85721-0026
520 626 8381
520 626 2976 fax
www.statemuseum.arizona.edu

MAY 4-6
Craven County Intertribal Powwow
Craven County Fairgrounds
New Bern NC
252 244 0357 Deborah Wayne
252 244 3312 fax
double d@coastalnet.com
ncnativenews@hotmail.com
http://ncnativenew.tripod.com

MAY 5
Harvard University Powwow
Location TBA
Cambridge MA
617 495 4923

MAY 5
Penn Cove Water Festival
Coupeville
Whidbey Island WA
360 679 7391

MAY 5
Native American Powwow
Spanaway Lake High School
Bethel WA
253 843 1175 Carol Dittbenner

 # MAY

MAY 5-6
Spring Corn Festival
Lenni Lenape Historical Society
Museum of Indian Culture
Allentown PA
610 797 2121

MAY 5-6
Creek Removal Commemorative Ride &
Festival
Ride from Ft Toulouse to Tuscumbia
Landing (Approximately. 235 miles)
Festival: Big Spring Park
Tuscumbia AL
205 672 0361 Perry White
256 773 7611 Larry Smith
877 818 3120 Toll Free
256 773 0911 fax
socolors@aol.com

MAY 5-6
Winona State University Intertribal
Powwow
Prairie Island Campground
Winona MN
507 454 6987 Bryce

First Saturday in MAY
Traditional Graduation Powwow
University of Manitoba
Winnipeg Manitoba
Canada
204 474 8850

First Weekend in MAY
Lords of the Plains Intertribal Contest
Powwow
Childress TX
940 937 2567

First Weekend in MAY
Eastern Kentucky Seventh Generation
Benefit Powwow
Old Time Machinery Grounds
Grayson KY
606 652 9850 Donna Church
606 652 4160 Christine Perkins

First Weekend in MAY
Crow Tribe Seniors Handgame
Tournament
Crow Agency MT
406 638 2601

MAY

Sun	Mn	Tue	We	Thr	Fri	Sat
		1	2	3	4	5
6	7	8	9	10	11	12
13	14	15	16	17	18	19
20	21	22	23	24	25	26
27	28	29	30	31		

First Weekend in MAY
Native American Indian Association
Powwow
Veterans Park
Charlotte NC
704 535 4419
www.indiantrailonline

First Weekend in MAY
American Indian Celebration
Knox Co Farmers Market
Knoxville TN
865 579 1384

First Weekend in MAY
Chemawa Birthday Powwow
Chemawa Indian School
Salem OR
503 399 5721 ext 260
mreyes@chemawa.bia.edu

First Weekend in MAY
Honor Mother Earth Powwow
Delboy Field
Rt 16 (Alewife Brook Parkway)
Sommerville MA
978 546 8161 Jackie Emerton

First Weekend in MAY
American Indian & World Culture
Festival
Mission San Juan Bautista
San Juan Bautista CA
831 623 2379 Sonny or Elaine Reyna

MAY 5-6
UCLA Powwow
Intermural Field
Los Angeles CA
310 206 7513 Crystal Roberts, Powwow
Director
310 206 7060 fax
cdk79@hotmail.com
www.sscnet.ucla.edu/indian/powwow.htm

 # MAY

MAY 10-13
Augusta Powwow
Camp Linwood Haynes
Hwy 56
Augusta GA
706 771 1221 Billy Medeiros
krazywilly@mindspring.com

MAY 11-13
Mothers Day Powwow
Withlacoochee River Park
Dade City FL
352 583 3388
352 567 0264

MAY 11-13
Cedar Cottage Traditional Powwow &
Mother's Day Celebration
Trout Lake Community Center
4065 Victoria Drive
Vancouver BC CANADA
604 874 4231

MAY 11-13 and MAY 18-20
Cherokee County Powwow
Cherokee County
Canton GA
770 735 6275

MAY 12
Spring Celebration Powwow
Quinn Coliseum
Eastern Oregon State College
La Grande OR 97850
541 962 3741 Trish Lewis
native@eou.edu

MAY 12
Native Graduate Powwow
Sumner High School
Sumner WA
800 664 4549 Martha Sherman

MAY 12
Running the Red Road
10K 5K Fun Run/Walk, 1K Children's Run
Balboa Park
San Diego CA
619 641 4133 Lucinda Millar
619 641 2377

MAY 12
Occoneechee State Park Heritage Annual
Festival and Powwow
Occoneechee State Park (Take Hwy 58 to
Kerr Lake)
Clarksville VA
Dancers & traders by invitation only
804 374 2436
919 304 3723 Tribal Office
occaneechi@visionet.org
tcouncil@up.net
www.occaneechi-saponi.org/

MAY 12-13
Native American Arts Festival &
Mother's Powwow
Riverside Park
Grants Pass OR
541 839 6704
541 474 6394

MAY 12-13 (Tentative)
Maui Powwow
War Memorial Park
Honolulu HI
808 947 3206 Bill Tiger
hawaiiich@aol.com   43

MAY 12-13
Traditional Sobriety Powwow
Cermak Pool Woods
7700 W Ogden Ave
Lyons IL
630 695 1292 Susan Malone
773 261 7501 Mike Pamonicutt
630 837 1240 fax
nativenationsinc@yahoo.com

MAY 12-13
Comanche Little Ponies Annual
Celebration
Lawton OK
580 429 8229 Robert Tippeconnie
lowelln@affiliatedtrans.com

Second Sunday MAY
Mothers Day All Indian Rodeo
Browning MT
406 338 7521

Mothers Day Weekend (MAY 12-13)
Satus Longhouse Powwow
Satus Longhouse Arbor
Satus WA
509 865 5121 Yakama Tourism
509 865 7570 fax

Mothers Day Weekend (MAY 12-13)
Respect One Another Mariposa Powwow
Mariposa Fairgrounds
Mariposa CA
209 966 5229 Sandy Chapman

Mothers Day Weekend (MAY 12-13)
Powwow
Dartmouth Green
Rain site: Thompson Arena
Hanover NH
603 646 2110

MAY 18-20
Northern Arapaho Tribal Housing & Drug
Elimination Spring Powwow
Arapahoe WY
800 433 0662

MAY 18-20
Tunica-Biloxi Powwow
Marksville LA
800 946 1946 ext 2034
tunica40@aol.com

MAY 18-20 and MAY 11-13
Cherokee County Powwow
Cherokee County
Canton GA
770 735 6275

Sun	Mn	Tue	We	Thr	Fri	Sat
	1	2	3	4	5	
6	7	8	9	10	11	12
13	14	15	16	17	18	19
20	21	22	23	24	25	26
27	28	29	30	31		

MAY

MAY 18-20
Medicine Ways Conference and Powwow
Univ of Cal-Riverside
Riverside CA
909 787 4143 Earl Sisto

MAY 18-20
Midlands Intertribal Powwow
Sate Fair Grounds
Columbia SC
803 772 9132 Marty McKinney

MAY 19
In Honor of Our Children Powwow
Kelso WA
360 577 2734 Judy Duff
360 636 4378 vendor info Pam Davis

Third Weekend in MAY
Tuscarora Nation of NC Powwow
Cory Road
Maxton NC
910 844 3352

Third Weekend in MAY
De Anza College Powwow & Arts Fair
21250 Steven Creek Road
Cupertino CA
408 864 5448
www.deanzapowwow.org

Third Weekend in MAY
Listen Together Youth Conference and
Powwow
Toppenish WA
509 865 5121 ext. 4451 Pat Goudy

Third Weekend in MAY
St. Croix Casino Spring Powwow
Hwy 63 & 8 W. of Turtle Lake
Turtle Lake WI
800 846 8946 ext 3046

Third Weekend MAY
Mat'Alyma Root Feast & Powwow
Kamiah ID
208 935 2525

Third Weekend in MAY
San Diego American Indian Cultural
Days
Balboa Park
San Diego CA
619 281 5964

MAY 19-20
Monaca Indian Powwow
Rte 130
Elon VA
804 946 0389

MAY 19-20
Richmond Community College Native
American Powwow
Richmond Community College Campus
Hamlet NC
910 582 7000 Wanda

MAY 19-20
Kiowa Black Leggings Ceremonial
Lone Bean Dance Grounds
Anadarko OK
405 247 6651
405 247 6652 fax

MAY

MAY 19-20
UNACC Annual Powwow
Fort Devens
Ayer MA
978 772 1306

MAY 19-20
East Hickman Powwow Festival
Hwy 100
Lyles TN
931 670 5465 Sheila

MAY 22-25
Aboriginal Awareness Week
Throughout Canada
613 957 3362 Carol Rhine

MAY 25-27
Memorial Day Powwow
Ceremonial Grounds
Cherokee NC
888 291 0632

MAY 25-27
Wyoming Indian High School Powwow
Ethete WY
800 433 0662

MAY 26
Southern California Indian Storytelling
Festival
Sherman Indian High School
9401 Oak Glen Rd
Riverside CA
510 794 7253 Lauren Teixeira
cistory@cistory.org
www.cistory.org

MAY 26
Upper Mattaponi Spring Festival &
Powwow
Upper Mattaponi Tribal Grounds
King William VA
804 769 4767

MAY 26-28
Spring Planting Moon Powwow
Topsfield Fairground
Topsfield MA
617 884 4227

MAY 26-SEP 23
Enduring Creations: Masterworks of
Native American and Regional Traditions
Museum of Northern Arizona
Flagstaff AZ
520 774 5213 ext 273
520 779 1527 fax
kmorehouse@mna.mus.az.us

MAY

Sun	Mn	Tue	We	Thr	Fri	Sat
	1	2	3	4	5	
6	7	8	9	10	11	12
13	14	15	16	17	18	19
20	21	22	23	24	25	26
27	28	29	30	31		

MAY

MAY 28
Yellow Calf Memorial Powwow
Ethete WY
800 433 0662

MAY 28-JUN 1
Indian Summer Day Camp
Meet at Smith Hall, University of
Alabama campus; transportation is pro-
vided to and from Moundville
Archaeological Park
Tuscaloosa AL
205 371 2234 Angie Jones
205 371 4180 fax
bbomar@bama.ua.edu (Bill Bomar)
moundvilee.ua.edu

Memorial Day Weekend (Tentative)
Gathering of People Powwow
Seabrook Elementary School
Seabrook NH
603 474 5259

Memorial Day Weekend (MAY 26-28)
Spring Powwow
Cass Lake MN
218 335 8289

Memorial Day Weekend (MAY 26-28)
Odawa Powwow
Nepean Tent & Trailer Park
411 Corkstown Road
Nepean ONT Canada
613 722 3811
www.odawa.com

Memorial Day Weekend (MAY 26-28)
Iroquois Indian Festival
Iroquois Indian Museum
Howes Cave NY
518 296 8949
www.iroquoismuseum.org

Memorial Day Weekend (MAY 26-28)
DE-UN-DA-GA Powwow
Meadville PA
412 882 0613

Memorial Day Weekend (MAY 26-28)
NAI Center Memorial Day Powwow
Ft Hayes
Columbus OH
614 443 6120
NAICCO@aol.com

Memorial Day Weekend (MAY 26-28)
Jemez Red Rocks Arts & Crafts Show
Jemez Pueblo NM
800 766 4405
505 834 7235

Memorial Day Weekend (MAY 26-28)
Cherokee Indian Festival
Ambler Campus
Temple University
Ambler PA
215 549 0828

Memorial Day Weekend (MAY 26-28)
Abenaki Celebration Powwow
Swanson VT or TBA
802 868 2559 Tribal Council
ashai@together.net

MAY

Memorial Day Weekend (MAY 26-28)
Mohawk Trail Powwow
Indian Plaza Mohawk Trail Rte 2
Charlemont MA
413 339 4096

Memorial Day Weekend (MAY 26-28)
Spring Juried Arts Festival
Rankocus Indian Reservation
Rancocas NJ
609 261 4747
609 261 7313 fax
www.powhatan.org

Memorial Day Weekend (MAY 26-28)
American Indianist Society (AIS) May
Dance
4-H Camp Marshall off Rte 31
Spencer MA
978 456 9707

Memorial Day Weekend (MAY 26-28)
Native American Warrior Society
Blackhawk Band Powwow
River Edge St
Yonkers NY
914 664 0974
914 668 5493

Memorial Day Weekend (MAY 26-28)
Two Rivers Powwow
Two Rivers Casino
Davenport WA 99122
509 722 4000 Robin Kieffer

Memorial Day (MAY 28)
Ohio Valley Memorial Day Powwow
Hocking College
Nelsonville OH
740 529 5322 Ray

MAY 28-31
Memorial Day Powwow
Lower Creek Muscogee Tribe
3733 Hwy 2321
Lynn Haven FL
850 763 6717 Chief Woods

MAY 31-JUN 3
Mill Bay Casino Annual Powwow/Rodeo
Event
455 Wapato Lake Road
Manson WA 98831
800 648 2946
509 687 4501 fax

MAY

Sun	Mn	Tue	We	Thr	Fri	Sat
		1	2	3	4	5
6	7	8	9	10	11	12
13	14	15	16	17	18	19
20	21	22	23	24	25	26
27	28	29	30	31		

JUN Date TBA
Lac Courte Oreilles Ojibwe School
Contest Powwow
La Courte Oreilles Ojibwe Reservation 10
miles SE of Hayward WI
715 634 8924 Charlene Larson
715 634 6058 fax

JUN Date TBA
Crow Heart Powwow
Crow Heart WY
307 337 9106

JUN Date TBA
Pi-Ume-Sha Days
Warm Springs OR
541 553 2461

JUN Date TBA
Soboba Casino Intertribal Powwow
San Jacinto CA
909 654 2765

JUN Date TBA
Stommish Water Festival
Lummi Stommish Grounds
15 miles NW via I-5 exit 260 to WA 540
Ferndale WA
360 384 2393 Mary Lou

MAY 31-JUN 3
Mill Bay Casino Annual Powwow/Rodeo
455 Wapato Lake Road
Manson WA 98831
800 648 2946
509 687 4501 fax

JUN 1-3
Otsiningo Powwow
Otsiningo Park. Exit 5, Interstate 81
Binghamton NY
607 729 0016 Dolores Elliott

JUN 1-3
Tulalip Veteran's Powwow
Tulalip Tribal Center
Marysville WA
360 651 4470 David C Fryberg

JUN 1-3
Honoring of the Elders Gathering
Mount Madonna Park
Top of Hecker Pass (Hwy 152)
Gilroy CA
408 258 1326 Jody

First Saturday in JUN
Corn Dance
Tesuque Pueblo NM
800 766 4405

JUN 2
Navajo Song & Dance
Ellis Tanner Trading Company
Gallup NM
800 233 4528
gitica@gallupceremonial.org

JUN 2-3
Triangle Native American Society
Powwow
State Farmer's Market
Raleigh NC
919 779 5936

JUN 2-3
Grand Village of the Kickapoo Park
Annual Powwow
Grand Village of the Kickapoo Park
RR 2
Leroy IL
309 962 2700 Bill or Doris Emmett
309 962 2701 fax
ccranch@davesworld.net
http://homepage.davesworld.net/~ccranch

JUN 2-3
Northern Colorado Intertribal Powwow
Association Annual Contest Powwow
McMillan Building
Larimer County Fairgrounds
700 S. Railroad Avenue
Loveland CO
970 226 4209
970 663 9240
ncipa@fortnet.org
http://www.fortnet.org/PowWow/

JUN 2-3
Kitigan Zibi Anishinabeg Traditional
Powwow
Kitigan Zibi Campgrounds
Maniwaki Quebec Canada
819 449 5449 Pauline Decontie

JUN 2-3
Cultural Festival & Powwow
Mattamuskeet Tribal Grounds
3085 Uniontown Road
Jamesville NC
252 793 1359 Carolyn Pierce

JUNE 2-3
Worchester Intertribal Center Powwow
Rutland State Park
Rutland MA
508 754 4994

First Weekend in JUN
Yuba Sutter Powwow
Yuba College
Marysville CA
530 749 6196

First Weekend in JUN
MIHS Powwow
American Indian Cultural Center
Waldorf, MD
301-372 1932
301 782 7622
mdindians@aol.com

JUNE

Sun	Mn	Tue	We	Thr	Fri	Sat
					1	2
3	4	5	6	7	8	9
10	11	12	13	14	15	16
17	18	19	20	21	22	23
24	25	26	27	28	29	30

 # JUNE

First Weekend in JUN
Alabama Coushatta Powwow
17 miles east of
Livingston TX
936 563 4391

JUN 8-10
Will Rogers Indian Club Powwow
Ellis O Jackson Park
Marshfield MO
417 256 4698
417 759 2782

JUN 8-10
Thunderbird Society Powwow
Belle MO
573 373 5566 Rosemary Dodd

JUN 8-10
Treaty Days Celebration
              —parade, powwow, and rodeo
Toppenish and White Swan, WA
509 865 5121 ext. 4750 Theresa Washlines

JUN 8-10
Red Earth Festival
Myriad Convention Center
Oklahoma City OK
405 427 5228
405 427 8079 fax
redearth@redearth.com
www.redearth.org

JUN 8-10
Waswanipi Traditional Powwow
Waswanipi Quebec Canada
819 753 2587 Lily Sutherland
819 753 2555 fax

JUN 9
Annual Native American Music Festival
Navajo Community College
Tsaile AZ
520 724 6741
520 724 6743

Second Weekend in JUN
Wollomononuppoag Indian Council
Powwow
La Salette Shrine Fairgrounds
Attleboro MA
508 822 5492

Second Weekend in JUN
White Earth Powwow
White Earth MN
218 983 3285 Gary

Second Weekend in JUN
Lenni Lenape Nanticoke Powwow
Salem Fairgrounds
Salem NJ
732 222 3638

Second Weekend in JUN
Occaneechei Saponi Spring Cultural
Festival and Powwow
On the Eno River
Hillsborough NC
919 304 3723 Tribal Office
occaneechi@visionet.org
tcouncil@up.net
www.occaneechi-saponi.org/

 # JUNE

Second Weekend in JUN
Indian Fair
Museum of Man
Balboa Park
San Diego CA
619 239 2001

Second Weekend in JUN
Intertribal Powwow
San Luis Rey Band of Mission Indians
Oceanside CA
760 724 8505 Carmen Majado

Second Weekend in JUN
Barrie Powwow
Barrie Fairground
Barrie ONT Canada
705 721 7689

Second Full Weekend in JUN
Lower Sioux Traditional Powwow
Lower Sioux Reservation
Morton MN
507 697 6185

JUN 9-10
Native American Indian Powwow
Indian Plaza
Rte 2 Mohawk Trail
Clarlemont MA
413 339 4096

JUN 13
San Antonio Feast Day
Corn Dance—Taos Pueblo NM
Corn Dance—Sandia Pueblo NM
Comanche Dance—Santa Clara Pueblo NM
505 843 7270

JUN 15-16
Ceremonial Intertribal Powwow
Location TBA
Gallup NM
800 233 4528

JUN 15-16
Intertribal Indian Ceremonial Powwow
Location TBA
Gallup NM
800 233 4528
gitica@gallupceremonial.org

JUN 15-16
AICA Traditional Powwow
Van Hoy Family Campground
Union Grove NC
704 464 5579 Ed

JUN 15-17
Khowutzun's "Thunder In The Valley"
Contest Powwow
Cowichan Community Center Area
2687 James St
Duncan Vancouver Island BC CANADA
250 748 9404 Harold Joe (Duncan)
604 253 1020 Kat Norris (Vancouver)

JUN 15-17
Arapaho Community Powwow
Arapahoe WY
800 433 0662

JUN 15-17
Eastern Delaware Nations Powwow
Forksville Fairgrounds-Sullivan Co
Forksville PA
570 924 9082
http://sites.netscape.net/lynsanders/edn

JUN 16
Mattaponi Indian Reservation Annual
Powwow
Mattaponi Indian Reservation
King William County VA
804 769 7745 Mattaponi Heritage
Foundation
804 769 0294 fax
leagle@inna.net

Third Saturday in JUN
Salmon Ceremony
Tulalip Tribal Grounds
Tulalip WA
360 651 4000

Third Weekend in JUN
Red Bottom Powwow
Ft Peck Reservation
Frazer MT
406 768 5155

Third Weekend in JUN
Twin Buttes Celebration
Twin Buttes ND
701 938 4396

Third Weekend in JUN
Chief Joseph & Warriors Memorial
Powwow
Lapwai ID
208 843 5901 Chloe Halfmoon

Third Weekend in JUN
Creek Nation Festival & Rodeo
Okmulgee OK
918 756 8700

Third Weekend in JUN
Quinn River Indian Rodeo
Ft McDermitt Reservation
McDermitt NV
775 532 8259

Third Weekend in JUN
Ring Thunder Traditional Powwow
Ring Thunder Community
11 miles NW of Mission SD
605 747 2316 Rose Stenstrom
605 856 2538
605 867 4115 fax

Third Weekend in JUN
Two Worlds Intertribal Lodge Gathering
Benson Farm
Stanwood MI
616 344 7111
polttwil@voyager.net

JUN 16-17
Plains Indian Powwow
Buffalo Bill Historical Center
Cody WY
307 578 4049

Father's Day Weekend (16-17)
Gateway to the Nations Powwow
Ft Hamilton Military Base
Brooklyn NY
718 686 9297

Father's Day Weekend (16-17)
Father's Day Powwow
Stewart Indian School Museum
Carson City NV
775 882 6929

Father's Day Weekend (16-17)
American Indian Center's Contest
Powwow
Edgewater Park
Cleveland OH
216 281 8480

 # JUNE

Father's Day Weekend (16-17)
Naes College Contest Powwow
Mather Park
Corner of California & Peterson Ave
Chicago IL
773 761 5000

Father's Day Weekend (16-17)
Worchester Indian Cultural Art Lodge
Powwow
Pratt Junction off Rte 12
Sterling MA
508 754 3300

Father's Day Weekend (16-17)
Wepawaug River's Indigenous Folk
Festival
Eisenhower Park
Milford CT
203 877 2811

Father's Day Weekend (16-17)
Kaskaskia River Dancer's Powwow
Peterson Park
Mattoon IL
217 234 7555 Pat

Father's Day Weekend (16-17)
Rebirth of the Traditional Spiritual
Gathering
North Carolina Indian Cultural Center
Pembroke NC
910 521 4178

Father's Day Weekend (16-17)
All Indian Rodeo
Birch Creek MT
406 472 3374 Wanda England

JUN 20-24
Grand Celebration
Grand Casino
Hinkley MN
800 472 6321

JUN 21
National Aboriginal Day
Throughout Canada
819 953 6163 Pat Baron
www.aboriginalday.com

JUNE

Sun	Mn	Tue	We	Thr	Fri	Sat
					1	2
3	4	5	6	7	8	9
10	11	12	13	14	15	16
17	18	19	20	21	22	23
24	25	26	27	28	29	30

A Catalog of Native American Books & Tapes

History	Wisdom
Culture	Contemporary Issues
Crafts	Children's Books
Women	Music & Video
Legends/Spiritualism	

Free Catalog:

Native Voices

P.O. Box 180
Summertown, TN 38483

1-800-695-2241

JUNE

JUN 21
National Aboriginal Day Art and Culture
Celebration
Vancouver Art Gallery Front Lawn Area
Vancouver BC Canada
604 684 2532 Germaine Langan
604 951 8861 fax
langan@netcom.ca

JUN 21
Shoshone Treaty Day
Fort Washakie WY
800 433 0662
307 337 9106

JUN 22-23
Intertribal Festival
Cherokee of Hoke County
Rockfish near Davis Bridge NC
910 875 0222 Chief or Mrs Edgar

JUN 22-24
Ft Randall Casino Contest Powwow
Wagner SD
800 362 6333 Sharon

JUN 22-24
Earth Speaks
Larado Taft
Oregon IL
815 753 0722 Rita
815 753 6366 fax
rreynolds@niu.edu

JUN 22-24
Oglala Lakota College Powwow
7 miles SW of
Kyle SD
605 455 2321

JUN 22-24 (Tentative)
Southeastern Michigan Indians Inc
Powwow
Gibralter Trade Center
Mt Clements MI
810 756 1350

JUN 22-24
Heber Valley Intertribal Powwow
100 South/1000 West
Heber City UT
801 595 1926 Trish Aperges
801 699 5548

JUNE

Sun	Mn	Tue	We	Thr	Fri	Sat
					1	2
3	4	5	6	7	8	9
10	11	12	13	14	15	16
17	18	19	20	21	22	23
24	25	26	27	28	29	30

JUNE

JUN 22-24
Shoshone Indian Days Powwow & Rodeo
Fort Washakie WY
800 433 0662

JUN 22-24
Great Lakes Powwow
On Reservation
Hannahville MI
906 466 2342

JUN 23-24
Eiteljorge Museum Indian Market
Indianapolis IN
317 636 9378

JUN 23-24
NENAI Spiritual Gathering
Sterling Spring Campground (call to confirm)
Sterling MA
508 886 6073 (no selling)

JUN 23-25
St Francis Indian Day Celebration
St Francis SD
605 856 2538
605 867 4115 fax

JUN 24
San Juan Feast Day
Taos Pueblo NM
800 766 4405

JUN 25-JUL 4
Ten Day Encampment Powwow
White Swan WA
509 874 2979 Virginia Harrison

JUN 29
San Pedro Feast Day
San Ana Pueblo NM
800 766 4405

JUN 29-JUL 1
Mt Tum Tum Native American
Encampment
Territorial Park
Amboy WA
360 423 6205 Tina Cummings
503 233 6823

Last Weekend in JUN
Powwow
Community Center
Sarnia ONT Canada
519 336 8410

JUN 30-JUL 1
Red Cliff Traditional Powwow
Red Cliff WI
715 779 3152
715 779 3387 Powwow Committee
715 779 5437 vendor info
715 779 5046 fax

JUN 30-JUL 1
Hopi Market Place
Museum of Northern Arizona
Flagstaff AZ
520 774 5213 Kari Morehouse
520 779 1527 fax
kmorehouse@mna.mus.az.us
360 687 0201 Toni

JULY

JUL Date TBA
Wukwemdong Sashoodenong Powwow
Kettle & Stony Point
ONT Canada
519 786 6680 Sharon Henry

JUL Date TBA
Little Eagle Powwow
Little Eagle ND
605 823 2081

JUL Date TBA
World Eskimo/Indian Olympics
Fairbanks AK
907 452 6646

JUL Date TBA
Mashpee Wampanoag Powwow
Mashpee Wampanoag Indian Tribal
Council
Barnstable County Fairgrounds
Rte 151
Mashpee/Falmouth Town Line MA
508 477 0208

JUL Date TBA
Ho Chunk Casino Powwow
Baraboo WI 53913
800 294 9343 ext 213

JULY Date TBA
Nespelem Celebration Powwow & All
Indian Rodeo
Nespelem WA
509 634 4711

JUL Date TBA
Columbia River Annual Powwow and
Encampment
Roosevelt Park
Roosevelt WA
509 865 5121 Yakama Tourism
509 865 7570 fax

JUL Date TBA
Missouri State Powwow
State Fairgrounds
Sedalia MO
660 826 5608

JUN 25-JUL 4
Ten Day Encampment Powwow
White Swan WA
509 874 2979 Virginia Harrison

JUN 29-JUL 1
Mt Tum Tum Native American
Encampment
Territorial Park
Amboy WA
360 423 6205 Tina Cummings
503 233 6823

JUN 30-JUL 1
Red Cliff Traditional Powwow
Red Cliff WI
715 779 3152
715 779 3387 Powwow Committee
715 779 5437 vendor info
715 779 5046 fax

JUN 30-JUL 1
Hopi Market Place
Museum of Northern Arizona
Flagstaff AZ
520 774 5213 Kari Morehouse
520 779 1527 fax
kmorehouse@mna.mus.az.us

JUL 1-2
Shawnee Nation URB Southwind Park
Fair
Zane Shawnee Caverns   St Rt 540
Bellefontaine OH
937 592 9592
937 592 4458 fax

JUL 4
Iron Lightning Powwow
Iron Lightning SD
605 964 4094

JUL 1-4
Lodge Grass Mid Summer Powwow
Lodge Grass MT
406 638 2601

JUL 1-31
Competitive Art Show
Five Civilized Tribes Museum
Muskogee OK 74401
918 683 1701 Clara Reekie
918 683 3070 fax
the5tribesmuseum@azalea.net
www.fivetribes.com

JUL 4
Nambe Waterfall Celebration
Nambe Pueblo NM
800 766 4405

JUL 4th Holiday
Bear Soldier Powwow
McLaughlin SD
701 854 7202

JULY 4th Weekend
July 4th Powwow
Ceremonial Grounds
Cherokee NC
888 291 0632

JULY 4th Weekend
Traditional Chippewa Powwow
Shunk Rd Powwow Grounds
Sault Ste Marie MI
906 635 6080 George Snider

JULY

Sun	Mn	Tue	We	Thr	Fri	Sat
1	2	3	4	5	6	7
8	9	10	11	12	13	14
15	16	17	18	19	20	21
22	23	24	25	26	27	28
29	30	31				

JULY 4th Weekend
Fourth of July Rodeo & Powwow
Window Rock AZ
520 871 6478

JULY 4th Weekend
Annual Fourth of July Celebration
Arlee MT
406 675 2700

JULY 4th Weekend
Spring Creek Veterans Memorial &
Survival Akicita
Spring Creek 10 miles west of St Francis
SD
605 856 2538
605 867 4886 fax

JULY 4th Weekend
Northern Cheyenne Powwow
Lame Deer MT
406 477 6284

JULY 4th Weekend
4th of July Rodeo and Powwow
Duck Valley Reservation
Owyhee NV
775 757 3211

JULY 4th Weekend
Wakpamni Lake Powwow
Batesland SD
605 867 5287

JULY 4th Weekend
Quapaw Tribal Powwow
Beaver Springs Park
Quapaw OK
918 542 1853

JULY 4th Weekend
4th of July Powwow
Memorial Grounds
Cass Lake MN
218 335 8289

JULY 4th Weekend
Oneida Powwow
Norbert Hill Center
Oneida WI
800 236 2214

First Weekend in JUL
Antelope Fair & Wacipi
Antelope Community
Mission SD
605 856 2538
605 867 4886 fax

First Weekend in JUL
Munsee-Delaware Nation Traditional
Gathering
Jubilee Road
Munsee-Delaware Nation
519 289 5475 Leo Nicholes
519 289 5049 fax

JUL 6-8
Wildhorse Casino Powwow
Wildhorse Powwow Grounds
Pendleton OR
800 654 9453 Michelle Liberty
541 276 6169 fax
info@wildhorseresort.com
www.wildhorseresort.com

JULY 7-8
Sussex Co Powwow
Sussex Co Fairgrounds
Augusta NJ
718 686 9297

JUL 7-8
Native American Indian Powwow
Indian Plaza
Rte 2 Mohawk Trail
Charlemont MA
413 339 4096

JUL 7-8
Powwow on the Hudson
Terrydock
Yonkers NY
914 664 0974
914 668 5493

JUL 11
Mini-Friendship Powwow
Bishop Hare Complex
Mission SD
605 856 4982

JUL 11-14
Calgary Stampede Indian Events
Powwow
Stampede Park
Calgary AB Canada
800 661 1260

JUL 13-15
Neesh-La Powwow
Baraboo WI
800 294 9343

JUL 13-15
Great Mohican Indian Powwow
Mohican Reservation Campgrounds
Loudonville OH
419 994 4987 Allen Combs
www.mohicanreservation.com/powwow

JUL 13-15
Powwow
White Fish Bay
ONT Canada
807 226 5411 Farrell White

JUL 21-22
Native American Iroquois Veterans
Association (NAIVA)
Annual Powwow
Veterans Park
Salamanca NY
716 283 0084

JULY

Sun	Mn	Tue	We	Thr	Fri	Sat
1	2	3	4	5	6	7
8	9	10	11	12	13	14
15	16	17	18	19	20	21
22	23	24	25	26	27	28
29	30	31				

JULY

JUL 13-22
Great Northern Art Festival
Midnight Sun Recreation Complex
Inuvik NWT Canada
867 777 3536 Tanya Van Valkenburg
867 777 4445 fax
greatart@permafrost.com
www.greatart.nt.ca

JUL 14
Shoalwater Bay Sobriety Powwow
Shoalwater Bay Reservation
Tokeland WA
360 267 5301 Sabina Harris
360 267 6766

Second Weekend in JUL
First Light Singers Powwow
Route 116
Savoy MA
718 726 2684

Second Weekend in JUL
Prairie Island Powwow
15 miles north of Red Wing
Prairie Island MN
800 554 5473

Second Weekend in JUL
Pinoleville Indian Reservation Big Time
Cultural Awareness Gathering
850 Orr Springs Road
Ukiah CA
707 463 1454 Leona Williams, Tribal
Chairperson
707 463 6601 fax
council@pinoleville.org

Second Weekend in JUL
Sac & Fox Powwow
Stroud OK
918 968 3526

Second Weekend in July
Taos Powwow
Taos Pueblo NM
505 758 3883

Second Weekend in JUL
International Montour Powwow
Montour ID
208 383 0125 Betty Soward

Second Weekend in JUL
North American Indian Days
Browning MT
406 338 7521
406 338 7276

Second Weekend in JUL
Arikara Celebration & Powwow
White Shield ND
701 743 4244

Second Weekend in JUL
Narragansett & Pequot Nations Powwow
Crandell Farm
Westerly RI
401 364 1100

JUL 14-15 (call to confirm)
Return to Beaver Creek Powwow
Matarazzo Farms
Belvidere NJ
908 475 3872

 # JULY

JUL 14-15
Savoy Powwow
Route 116
Savoy MA
718 726 2684

JUL 14-15
RI Indian Council Powwow
Roger Williams Park
Providence RI
401 781 1098
401 781 1095 Chris

JUL 14-15
Howard Co Powwow
Howard Co fairgrounds
Friendship MD
252 257 5383

JUL 13-15
Nooksack Tribe's Genesis II Powwow
6750 Mission Road
Everson WA
360 966 7704

JUL 15-16
Eight Northern Indian Pueblos
Artists & Craftsman Show
San Ildefonso Pueblo NM
505 843 7270

JUL 16-17
Afraid of His Horse Ceremonial
Afraid of His Horse Memorial Park
Pine Ridge SD
605 867 5670
605 867 1223

JUL 18
Mini-Friendship Powwow
Bishop Hare Complex
Mission SD
605 856 4982

JUL 20-22
Ethete Powwow
Ethete WY
800 433 0662

JUL 20-29
Cheyenne Frontier Days
Frontier Park
Cheyenne WY
800 227 6336
www.cfdrodeo.com

Third Weekend in JUL
Honor the Elders Powwow
North Elementary School
Wetstone Road
Somerset MA
508 880 6887

Third Weekend in JUL
Five Nations Intertribal Powwow
Cherokee Nation of New Jersey
40th Street Park
Irvington NJ
973 374 1021 after 7 pm Chief C. W. Longbow
973 375 3049 Ed Sunwolf

Third Weekend in JUL
Big Bear All Nations Powwow
Los Vaqueros Rodeo Arena off Hwy 39 &
Zaca Rd
Big Bear City CA
909 584 7115
909 790 1390 Faye Roman
408 295 9509 Pegge Lemke

Third Weekend in JUL
Milk's Camp Traditional Wacipi
Powwow Grounds
St Charles/Bonesteel SD
605 856 2538
605 867 4886 fax

Third Weekend in JUL
Coburg Golden Years Powwow
Coburg OR
541 579 7238 Dennis Bancroft

Third Weekend in JUL
Flandreau Santee Sioux Wacipi
Flandreau SD
605 997 3891

Third Weekend in JUL
Little Beaver Powwow
Jicarilla Apache Tribe
Dulce NM
505 759 3242

Third Weekend in JUL
Mandaree Celebration & Powwow
Mandaree ND
701 759 3311

Third Weekend in JUL
Blackberry Jam Powwow
Lowell OR
541 687 3489 (Oct-May)
541 341 1384 Brenda

 # JULY

Third Weekend in JUL
Standing Arrow Powwow
Elmo MT
406 849 6018 Richard or Bernice

Third Weekend JUL
Mee-Gwitch Mahnomen
Powwow Grounds
Ball Club MN
218 335 8289

Third Weekend JUL
Chapel Island Powwow
Richmond NS Canada
902 535 3317

Third Weekend JUL
Native American Iroquois Veterans
Association (NAIVA) Annual Powwow
Veterans Park
Salamanca NY
716 283 0084

JUL 21-22
Native American Gathering & Powwow
Mt Kearsarge Indian Museum
Kearsarge Mt RD
Warner NH
603 456 2600

JUL 21-22
Champion of Champions Powwow
Chiefwoods Park
Grand River Reserve ONT Canada
519 758 5444

JUL 21-22
Tamkaliks Celebration
WBNPTIC Project Site
Wallowa OR
541 886 3101 Liam or Mary
541 886 3016 fax
WMP@oregonvos.net
wallowanezperce.org

JUL 25
Mini-Friendship Powwow
Bishop Hare Complex
Mission SD
605 856 4982

JUL 25
Santiago Feast Day
Taos Pueblo NM
800 766 4405

JUL 26
Santa Ana Feast Day
Santa Ana Pueblo NM
Taos Pueblo NM
505 843 7270

JULY

Sun	Mn	Tue	We	Thr	Fri	Sat
1	2	3	4	5	6	7
8	9	10	11	12	13	14
15	16	17	18	19	20	21
22	23	24	25	26	27	28
29	30	31				

JUL 27-29
Thunderbird Dancers Powwow
Queens County Farm Museum
73-50 Little Neck Parkway
Floral Park Queens NY
201 587 9633 Louis

JUL 27-29
Seafair Indian Days Powwow
Daybreak Star Center
Discovery Park
Seattle, WA
206 285 4425 Claudia Kauffman
info@unitedindians.com

JUL 28-29
Grand River Powwow
Six Nations Reserve
Ohsweken ONT Canada
519 445 4391 Evelyn

JUL 28-29
Listugu Powwow
Point Ala Croix
Quebec Canada
418 788 2136 Shelia Isaac
418 788 2058 fax

Fourth Weekend in JUL
Keweenaw Bay Traditional Powwow
Ojibwa Campground
Baraga MI
906 353 6623 Paulene or Terry

Last Weekend in JUL
Gagaguwon Traditional Indian Powwow
AuSable Children's Park
AuSable MI
517 739 1994 Joe Ireland

Last Weekend in JUL
Annual Sobriety Powwow
Auburn WA
253 939 3311 ext 153 Walter Pacheco
253 833 6177 fax

Last Weekend in JUL
Milk River Indian Days
Ft Belknap MT
406 353 2205

Last Weekend in JUL
Winnebago Homecoming
Veterans Park
Winnebago NE
402 878 2272

Last Weekend in JUL
Cowasuck Band of the Pennacook-
Abenaki Traditional Summer Gathering
Parlin Field (off Route 10)
Newport NH
508 528 7629
www.cowasuck.org

Last Sunday in JUL
St Ann Days
Belcourt ND
701 477 5601

JUL 29
Native American Fair & Powwow
Hassanamissitt Reservation
80 Brigham Hill Rd
Grafton MA
508 393 8860 Walter Vickus

 # AUGUST

AUG Date TBA
Huckleberry Feast
Warm Springs OR
541 553 3257

AUG Date TBA
Oglala Nation Powwow & Rodeo
Pine Ridge SD
605 867 5821

AUG Date TBA
Kalispel Salish Fair
Powwow Grounds
Usk WA
509 444 0211

AUG Date TBA
Ramapough-Lenape Powwow
Sally's Field
Ringwood NJ
201 529 1171
www.ramapoughnation.org/main.html

AUG Date TBA
Spirit of the Anishnawbe Powwow
Garden River First Nation
Sault Ste. Marie
ONT Canada
705 946 6300 Powwow Committee

AUG 1
Mini-Friendship Powwow
Bishop Hare Complex
Mission SD
605 856 4982

AUG 3-5
Sacramento Skins Annual Powwow
O'Neil Park
6th & Broadway
Sacramento CA
916 421 0657 Marcia

AUG 3-5
Lake of The Eagles Traditional Powwow
Eagle Lake First Nation
ONT Canada
807 755 5526

AUG 3-5
Wikwemikong Powwow
Manitoulin Island
ONT Canada
705 859 2385

AUG 4
Santo Domingo Feast Day
Santa Domingo Pueblo NM
800 766 4405

AUG 4-5
Saco River Intertribal Powwow
Hussey Field
River Road
North Conway NH
603 356 9075

AUG 4-5
Woodland Festival & Craft Show
Flying Airpark
Perth NY
518 762 1191

 # AUGUST

Abalone • Dentalium
Cowries • Olivella

Craft Shells for Indian Regalia
and Jewelry Manufacture • Hides

CHUCK AND BARBARA SNELL
P.O. Box 769, Trinidad, CA 95570
Phone/Fax 707-677-0460

Wholesale   Seller's Permit #SRJHB 99408847

AUG 4-5
Navajo Marketplace
Museum of Northern Arizona
3101 North Fort Valley Road
Flagstaff AZ 86001
520 774 5213 ext 273
520 779 1527 fax
kmorehouse@mna.mus.az.us

AUG 4-5
Nu'eta Count Buffalo Festival
Ft Abe Lincoln St Park
Mandan ND
701 663 1464

AUG Full Moon Weekend (AUG 4-5)
Umonhon Harvest Hethushka
Macy NE
402 837 5391

First Weekend in AUG
Aggie Fair Powwow
Bowefield Fairgrounds
Adams MA
718 726 2684

First Weekend in AUG
Native American Festival
Whiteface Mountain
Wilmington NY
518 946 4299

First Weekend in AUG
Shawnee Woodland Powwow
Zane Shawnee Caverns
7092 St Rt 540
Bellefontaine OH
937 592 9592
937 592 4458 fax

First Full Weekend in AUG
Ft Randall Powwow
Lake Andes SD
605 384 3641

AUGUST

First Weekend in AUG
Wososo Wakpala District Celebration
Wacipi Grounds Between He Dog &
Upper Cut Meat southwest of
Parmelee SD
605 856 2538
605 856 4886 fax

First Weekend in AUG
Wadopana Celebration
Wolf Point MT
406 653 1818

First Weekend in AUG
Dakota Wacipi
Upper Sioux State Park
Granite Falls MN
320 564 2360

First Weekend in AUG
Rocky Boy Powwow
Rocky Boy Agency
Havre MT
406 395 4478

First Weekend in AUG
United American Indians of Delaware
Valley Powwow
Playhouse In The Park
Fairmont Park PA
215 574 9020

First Weekend in AUG
Peigan Nation Celebration
Brocket AB Canada
403 965 3940

First Weekend in AUG
Standing Rock Wacipi
Fort Yates SD
701 854 7451

First Weekend in AUG
Kitsap Co. Indian Center Powwow
Erlands Point Road
Chico WA
360 876 0914 (vendor info)
kitsapcoindiancenter@yahoo.com

First Weekend in AUG
Southern California Powwow
Oragen County Fairgrounds
Costa Mesa CA
714 663 1102

First Weekend in AUG
Menominee Nation Contest Powwow
Woodland Bowl Powwow Grounds
Keshena WI
715 799 3341

AUGUST

Sun	Mn	Tue	We	Thr	Fri	Sat
				1	2	3	4
5	6	7	8	9	10	11
12	13	14	15	16	17	18
19	20	21	22	23	24	25
26	27	28	29	30	31	

AUG 6-11
American Indian Exposition
Caddo County Fairgrounds
Anadarko OK
405 247 6651 Debbie Riddle
405 247 6652 fax
chamber@tanet.net
www.indianexpo.org

AUG 8
Mini-Friendship Powwow
Bishop Hare Complex
Mission SD
605 856 4982

AUG 9
San Lorenzo Sunset Vespers
Picuris NM
505 843 7270

AUG 10
San Lorenzo Feast Day
Acomita NM
505 843 7270

AUG 10
San Lorenzo Feast Day Trade Fair &
Ceremonial Footrace
Picuris Pueblo NM
505 843 7270

AUG 10-12
Songhees Powwow
Victoria BC Canada
250 385 3938 Angela or Cheryl Joseph

AUG 10-12
Mohincan Veterans Powwow
Many Trails Park
Bowler WI
715 793 4111

AUG 10-12
Nesika Illahee Powwow
Pauline Ricks Memorial Powwow
Grounds
Siletz OR
800 922 1399 Craig Whitehead
541 444 2307 fax
craigw@ctsi.nsn.us

AUG 10-12
Thunderbird Society Powwow
Vandalia MO
573 874 3454

AUG 10-12
Sipayik Indian Day
Pleasant Point
Passamaquoddy Tribal Reservation
Perry ME
207 853 2600 Tribal Governor
207 853 6039 fax
www.nemaine.com/passamaquoddy

AUG 10-12
Omak Stampede
Omak WA
800 933 6625

Second Weekend in AUG
Lac Vieux Desert Powwow
Old Indian Village
Watersmeet MI
906 358 4577

Second Weekend in AUG
Lower Brule Fair & Powwow
Lower Brule SD
605 473 5399

 # AUGUST

Second Weekend in AUG
Mesquakie Powwow
Tama IA
515 484 4678

Second Weekend in AUG
Havasu Peace Festival
Supai AZ
520 448 2731

Second Weekend in AUG
IICOT Powwow
State Fairgrounds
Tulsa OK
918 836 1523

Second Weekend in AUG
Little Shell Powwow
New Town ND
701 627 4307
701 627 4781

Second Weekend in AUG
Heart Butte Society Celebration
Heart Butte MT
406 338 7521

AUG 11-12
Paumanauke Powwow
Copaigue Long Island NY
631 661 7559

AUG 11-12
Blue Water Indian Celebration/Contest
Powwow
Pine Grove Park
Port Huron MI
810 982 0891

AUG 11-12
Mihsihkinaahkwa Traditional Powwow
Morsches Park
Columbia City IN
219 982 7172 Sue Lester
219 625 4370 Cathy Mowrey (Vendors)
miamipowwow@kconline.net

AUG 12
Santa Clara Feast Day
Santa Clara Pueblo NM
505 843 7270

AUG 12
Roasting Ears of Corn Feast
Lenni Lenape Historical Society
Museum of Indian Culture
Allentown PA
610 797 2121

AUGUST

Sun	Mn	Tue	We	Thr	Fri	Sat
				1	2	3	4
5	6	7	8	9	10	11
12	13	14	15	16	17	18
19	20	21	22	23	24	25
26	27	28	29	30	31	

AUG 15
Mini-Friendship Powwow
Bishop Hare Complex
Mission SD
605 856 4982

AUG 15
Zia Pueblo Feast Day
Zia Pueblo NM
505 843 7270

AUG 15
Assumption of our Blessed Mother's
Feast Day
Laguna Pueblo NM
505 843 7270

AUG 16-19
Wichita Annual Dance
Wichita Tribal Park 1 mile N on Hwy
281
Anadarko OK
405 247 2425 ext 210
405 247 2430 fax
www.wichita.nsn.us

AUG 17-19
American Indian Hobbyist Powwow
Flying W Ranch
Kelletsville PA
412 331 6129 Tom Mance

AUG 17-19
Ponca Powwow
Niobrara NE
402 857 3519

AUG 17-19
Mille Lacs Traditional Powwow
Onamia MN
320 532 4181

AUG 17-19
Shakopee Mdewakanton Powwow
Prior Lake MN
612 445 8900

AUG 17-19
Mawiomi of Tribes Annual Powwow
Spruce Haven Aroostook County Park
Rte 1
Presque Isle ME
207 769 2103 Bernard Jerome

AUG 17-19
Intertribal Fest
Fort Robinson State Park
Campground
Fort Robinson NE
308 665 2900 Campground
303 279 2709 Robert White

AUG 17-20
Crow Fair
Crow Agency MT
406 638 2601 Burton Pretty On Top

AUG 18-19
Dawnland Center Intertribal Powwow
Henry Parker's Field
Rte 2
East Montpelier VT
802 229 0601 Patty

AUG 18-19
Texas Inter-Tribal Indian Organization
Homecoming Powwow
Amarillo National Events Bldg
Amarillo TX
806 358 3277 Billy Turpin, President
806 378 8082 fax

AUG 18-19
Santa Rosa Powwow
Sonoma County Fairgrounds
Santa Rosa CA
707 869 8233

AUG 18-19
AIC Traditional Powwow
Boone County 4-H Grounds
Lebanon IN
765 482 3315

AUGUST

Sun	Mn	Tue	We	Thr	Fri	Sat
			1	2	3	4
5	6	7	8	9	10	11
12	13	14	15	16	17	18
19	20	21	22	23	24	25
26	27	28	29	30	31	

AUGUST

AUG 18-20
Kamloopa Powwow
Special Events Facility Kamloops Indian
Band
Kamloops BC Canada
250 314 1535 Delyla Peters
250 314 1539 fax
www.mwsolutions.com/kib/

Third Weekend in AUG
Zuni Tribal Fair
Zuni NM
505 843 7270

Third Weekend in AUG
Traditional Powwow & Frontier Days
White River SD
605 856 2530

Third Weekend in AUG
Native American Indian Powwow
Indian Plaza, Rt 2 Mohawk Trail
Charlemont MA
413 339 4096

Third Weekend in AUG
Chief Looking Glass Powwow
Kamiah ID
208 935 2890 Nancy

Third Weekend in AUG
Piapot Indian Celebration & Powwow
Piapot Reserve SASK Canada
306 781 4848

Third Weekend in AUG
OSAWAN
Location TBA
Belvediere IL
815 436 4950

Third Weekend in AUG
Nansemond Indian Tribal Festival
Lone Star Lakes Lodge
Chuckatuck VA
757 421 3160 Debbie Smith

Third Weekend in AUG
Rocky River Rendezvous and Powwow
Memory Isle Park
Three Rivers MI
616 344 7111
polttwil@voyager.net

Third Weekend in AUG
Chief Seattle Days
Suquamish WA
206 598 3311

Third Weekend in AUG
Crow Creek Sioux Annual Powwow
Ft Thompson SD
605 245 2221
605 245 2470 fax

AUGUST

Third Weekend in AUG
Skopabsh Powwow & Celebration
Muckleshoot Reservation
Auburn WA
253 393 3311 ext 153 Walter Pacheco
253 833 6177 fax

AUG 19-20
Santa Fe Indian Market
Santa Fe Plaza & Vargas Mall
Santa Fe NM
505 983 5220

AUG 22
Mini-Friendship Powwow
Bishop Hare Complex
Mission SD
605 856 4982

AUG 23-26
Mashantucket Pequot Nation Annual
Schemitzun Powwow
Mashantucket CT
860 396 7070

AUG 24-26
Sac & Fox Casino Powwow
Hwy 75
Pwchattan KS
800 990 2946 ext 1018

AUG 24-26
West Valley City Powwow
Honoring Our Veterans
Granger Park
West Valley City UT 84119
801 973 2078 Harry James Sr
wscfam.hjames@state.ut.us

AUG 24-26
Spokane Falls Powwow
Riverfront Park
Spokane WA
509 535 0886

AUG 24-26
Baltimore Indian Center Powwow
Catonsville Community College
Baltimore MD
410 675 3535

AUG 25
Tonokwa Hills Blues Festival
Indian City Dance Grounds
Anadarko OK
405 247 6651
405 588 2356

AUGUST

Sun	Mn	Tue	We	Thr	Fri	Sat
			1	2	3	4
5	6	7	8	9	10	11
12	13	14	15	16	17	18
19	20	21	22	23	24	25
26	27	28	29	30	31	

AUG 25-26
GLICA Powwow
Lowell-Contucket Blvd
Lowell MA
978 667 6498 evenings

AUG 25-26
St. Joe's Indian School Annual Benefit
Bike Run and Powwow
Bike Run—AUG 25
Powwow—AUG 26
Ed Rehrer's Campground
Manada Bottom Road
Grantville PA
717 469 0362 Wendy or Joe

AUG 25-26
Traditional Summer Social
Potowatomi Trails
Zion IL
847 746 9086

Last Weekend in AUG
Annual Ponca Powwow
White Eagle Park
Ponca City OK
580 762 8104
poncatribe@concacity.net

Fourth Weekend in AUG
Fort Kipp Celebration & Powwow
American Legion Park
Poplar MT
406 448 2546

Fourth Weekend in AUG
Rosebud Fair & All Indian Rodeo
Rosebud SD
605 856 2538
605 856 4886 fax

Fourth Weekend in AUG
Spirit of Wovoka Days Powwow
Pat Peeples Softball Field
Yerington NV
775 463 2350

AUG 26-27
Inger Powwow
Inger MN
218 335 8289

AUG 31
Northern Arapaho Powwow
Arapahoe WY
800 433 0662

AUG 31-SEP 2
Weegitchienemedim Contest Powwow
Cass Lake MN
218 335 8289

AUG 31-SEP 2
Puyallup Tribal Powwow
2002 East 20th Street
Tacoma WA 9804
253 573 7800

AUG 31-SEP 3
Choctaw Nation Labor Day Festival
Tushkahomma OK
580 924 8280
bishinik@choctawnation.com
www.choctawnation.com

SONG STICK
NATIVE AMERICAN FLUTES AND MUSIC

HAND CRAFTED BY TROY DE ROCHE
AN ENROLLED MEMBER OF THE BLACKFEET NATION

EXPRESSING TRADITIONAL VALUES AND THE
SPIRITUAL NATURE OF NATIVE AMERICAN PEOPLE
THROUGH MUSIC

WWW.SONGSTICK.COM

BROCHURE $1.00

POST OFFICE BOX 490
CHIMACUM, WA. 98325

AUG 31-SEP 2
Weegitchienemedim Contest Powwow
Cass Lake MN
218 335 8289

AUG 31-SEP 2
Puyallup Tribal Powwow
2002 East 20th Street
Tacoma WA 9804
253 573 7800

AUG 31-SEP 3
Choctaw Nation Labor Day Festival
Tushkahomma OK
580 924 8280
bishinik@choctawnation.com
www.choctawnation.com

MAY 26-SEP 23
Enduring Creations: Masterworks of
Native American and Regional Traditions
Museum of Northern Arizona
Flagstaff AZ
520 774 5213 ext 273
520 779 1527 fax
kmorehouse@mna.mus.az.us

SEP Date TBA
Native Friendship Centre of Montreal
Traditional Powwow
Bonsecours Island in the Old Port of
Montreal Canada
514 499 1854

SEP Date TBA
American Indian Center Powwow
Queeny Park
St Louis MO
314 773 3316

SEP Date TBA
Annual Harvest Powwow
Immanuel Lutheran Church Picnic
Grounds
Mokena IL
630 961 9323

SEP-OCT Dates TBA
Moving Waters Powwow
River Valley Resort
Canyon Lake TX
830 964 3613 John Guenzel/Sue Nelson
830 964 3620 fax
rioraft@gvtc.com
www.rivervalleyresort.net

SEP 1-2
Zuni Market Place
Museum of Northern Arizona
Flagstaff AZ
520 774 5213 ext 273
520 779 1527 fax
kmorehouse@mna.mus.az.us

SEP 1-2
Running Water Powwow
Ridge Ferry Park
Rome GA
706 232 1714 Frank Blair after 5
fmblair@aol.com
geocities.com/heartland/6689

SEP 2
San Estevan Feast Day
Acoma Pueblo NM
505 843 7270

 # SEPTEMBER

First Weekend in SEP
Fiddling & Jigging Festival
Soaring Eagle Friendship Centre
Hay River NWT Canada
867 874 6581

Labor Day Weekend
Kee Boon Mein Kaa Powwow
St Patrick's Co Park
South Bend IN
616 782 1763

Labor Day Weekend
Alkali Lake Powwow
Williams Lake BC Canada
250 440 5626 Josephine

Labor Day Weekend
Michinemackinong Powwow
Carp River
St Ignace MI
906 863 9831

Labor Day Weekend
Ponemah Traditional Powwow
Ponemah MN
218 679 3341

Labor Day Weekend
Lake Shawnee Traditional Intertribal
Powwow
Lake Shawnee
Topeka KS
785 272 5489

Labor Day Weekend
Porcupine Powwow
Porcupine SD
605 867 5728

Labor Day Weekend
LIHA Annual Labor Day Powwow
Laconia Indian Historical Association
Dulac Land Trust
Sanbornton NH
603 437 3926

Labor Day Weekend
First Light Native American Gathering &
Festival
Academy Street
Athens ME
207 654 3981 Many Winds

SEPTEMBER

Sun	Mn	Tue	We	Thr	Fri	Sat
						1
2	3	4	5	6	7	8
9	10	11	12	13	14	15
16	17	18	19	20	21	22
23	24	25	26	27	28	29
30						

 # SEPTEMBER

Labor Day Weekend
Totah Festival Contest Powwow
Farmington Civic Center
Farmington NM
800 448 1240

Labor Day Weekend
Iroquois Indian Festival
Iroquois Indian Museum
Howes Cave NY
518 296 8949
www.iroquoismuseum.org

Labor Day Weekend
NAI Center Labor Day Powwow
Heimet Haus
Grove City OH
614 443 6120
NAICco@aol.com

Labor Day Weekend
White Mountain Apache Tribal Fair &
Rodeo
Fairgrounds
White River AZ
520 338 4346

Labor Day Weekend
Cheyenne River Sioux Fair & Rodeo
Eagle Butte SD
605 964 4426
605 964 1180 fax

Labor Day Weekend
Cherokee National Holiday
& Powwow
Cherokee Nation Powwow Grounds
Tahlequah OK
918 456 0671

Labor Day Weekend
Wee-Gitchie-Ne-Me-E-Dim Powwow
Leech Lake Reservation
Cass Lake MN
218 335 8289

Labor Day Weekend
Eufaula Powwow
Eastside Park
Eufaula OK
918 689 5066

Labor Day Weekend
Spokane Tribal Celebration
Powwow Grounds
Wellpinit WA
509 258 9114
509 258 8665 fax

Labor Day Weekend
Poplar Indian Day Powwow
Poplar MT
406 768 5155

Labor Day Weekend
Kla How Ya Days
Tulalip Tribal Grounds
Marysville WA
360 651 4000

Labor Day Weekend
Shinnecock Powwow
Shinnecock Reservation
Southhampton NY
631 283 6143

 SEPTEMBER

SEPTEMBER

Labor Day Weekend
Ottawa Powwow & Celebration
Adawe Park
Miami OK
918 540 1536

Labor Day Weekend
Tecumseh Lodge Powwow
Tipton 4-H Grounds
Tipton IN
317 773 4233
http://tlodge.srphoto.net

Labor Day Weekend
Pacific Coast Indian Club Powwow
Barona Indian Reservation
Lakeside CA
619 443 6612

Labor Day Weekend
Labor Day Weekend Powwow
Caddo Tribal Grounds 5 miles east of
Binger OK
405 656 2344

Labor Day Weekend
Native American Indian Powwow
Indian Plaza Rte 2 Mohawk Trail
Charlemont MA
413 339 4096

Labor Day Weekend
California Indian Market
Mission San Juan Bautista
San Juan Bautista CA
831 623 2379 Sonny or Elaine Reyna

Labor Day Weekend
Numuga Indian Days
Hungry Valley Community
Sparks NV
775 425 0775

Labor Day Weekend
Moraviantown Powwow
Exit 117 off 401
Moravian Reserve ONT Canada
519 692 3936

SEP 4
San Augustine Feast Day
Isteta Pueblo NM
505 843 7270

SEP 7-9
Seminole Nation Days Powwow
Mekusukey Mission
Seminole OK
405 380 2653
www.renet.com/semnat/

SEP 7-9
Trail of Tears Intertribal Powwow
Trail of Tears Park
Hopkinsville KY
270 886 8033 Beverly Baker
www.trailoftears.org

SEP 7-9
Precious Sunset Powwow
Recreation Point
Bass Lake CA
559 855 2705
559 855 2695 fax

84

SEP 8
Nativity of the Blessed Virgin Mary's
Feast Day
Laguna Pueblo (Encinal) NM
San Ildefonso Pueblo NM
505 843 7270

SEP 8-9
Coharie Powwow
7531 North US 421 Hwy
Clinton NC
910 564 6909

SEP 8-9
Chattanooga Indian Festival
Camp Jordon Park
Chattanooga TN
770 735 6275 Chipa Wolf

SEP 8-9
Nanticoke Indian Powwow
7 mi east Millsboro, 12 mi west Rte1
Millsboro DE
302 945 3400
302 945 7022

SEP 8-9
Mass Center for Native American
Awareness Annual Chief Red Blanket
Memorial Powwow
Plug Pond
Mill Street
Oxford MA
617 884 4227

SEP 8-10
Indian Summer Festival
Maier Festival Park Complex
Milwaukee WI 53214
414 774 7119
414 774 6810 fax
www.indiansummer.org

SEP 8-OCT 21
Lawrence Indian Arts Show
Haskell Indian Nations University
Lawrence KS
785 864 4245 Maria Martin
www.ukans.edu/~lias

Weekend after Labor Day (SEP 8-9)
Sycuan Powwow
El Cajon CA
619 445 7776 Arlene Galvan

Weekend after Labor Day (SEP 8-9)
United Tribes International Powwow
National Miss Indian Nations Pageant
Indian Art Expo
Bismark ND
701 255 3285

Second Weekend in SEP
Southern Ute Tribal Fair & Powwow
Sky Ute Downs
Ignacio CO
800 772 1236

Second Weekend in SEP
Chawbunagungamang Council Nipmuck
Powwow
Greenbriar Park Rte 12
Oxford MA
508 865 9828

Second or Third Weekend in SEP
Stone Lake Fiesta
Jacarilla Apache Reservation
Dulse NM
505 843 7270

Second Weekend in SEP
Salmon Homecoming Celebration
The Seattle Aquarium
Seattle WA
206 386 4300
seattleaquarium.org

SEPTEMBER

Sun	Mn	Tue	We	Thr	Fri	Sat
						1
2	3	4	5	6	7	8
9	10	11	12	13	14	15
16	17	18	19	20	21	22
23	24	25	26	27	28	29
30						

 # SEPTEMBER

Second Weekend in SEP
Twin Eagles Indian Powwow
8600 Buncombe Rd
Shreveport LA
318 933 8200
318 688 6980

SEP 9-10
Native American Appreciation Day &
Cultural Exchange Powwow
Topsham Fairgrounds (call to confirm)
Topsham ME
207 339 9520 Scotty Wilson

SEP 12-15
Pendleton Round Up
Pendleton OR
800 457 6336
www.ucinet.com/~roundup\ruticks.html

SEP 14-16
Mohican Indian Powwow
Mohican Reservation Campground
Loudonville OH
419 994 4987 Allen Combs
www.mohicanreservation.com/powwow

SEP 14-16
Indian Summer Festival
Community Center
Bartlesville OK
918 336 2787

Third Saturday in SEP
TIA-TIHA Benefit Dance
St Pius V Catholic Church
New Caney TX
713 475 0221 Dale Adams
Dadams2010@AOL.com
281 448 8435 Grant Gaumer

Third Weekend in SEP
Native American Indian Association
(NAIA) Powwow
Indian Trail Elementary
Indian Trail NC
704 535 4419

Third Weekend in SEP
Trail of Tears Commemorative Motor
Cycle Ride
Chatanooga TN to Waterloo AL
205 672 0361 Penny White

Third Weekend in SEP
AAIWV/ANI Homecoming
St Albans WV
304 683 3647 Mel C. / 253 0789 fax
wkngbear@cwvc.net

Third Weekend in SEP
Archeofest
Pinson Mounds
Pinson TN
901 988 5614

Third Weekend in SEP
Everything is Sacred Powwow
Borchard Community Park
Thousand Oaks CA
805 493 2863
805 493 2163 fax

 # SEPTEMBER

Third Weekend in SEP
Festival of Pai Arts
Museum of Northern Arizona
Flagstaff AZ
520 774 5213
520 779 1527 fax

Third Weekend in SEP
Guilford Native American Association
(GNAA) Powwow
Greensboro Country Park
Greensboro NC
336 273 8686

Third Weekend in SEP
Northern Sierra Indian Days
Greenville High School
Greenville CA
530 283 3402

Third Weekend in SEP
Honoring Our Elders Powwow & Pine
Nut Festival
Walker River Reservation
Schurz NV
775 773 2306

Third Weekend in SEP
California American Indian Days
Celebration
Balboa Park
San Diego CA
619 281 5964

Third Weekend in SEP
GLICA & Bedford VA Hospital Powwow
200 Springs RD
Bedford MA
978 667 6498

Third Weekend in SEP
Paw Paw Moon Festival Powwow
George Rogers Clark Park
Springfield OH
937 663 4345

SEP 15-16
Four Winds Powwow
Killeen Special Events Center
3301 South W.S. Young
Killeen TX
254 699 3167 Paula Brock
254 699 3038 fax
www.fourwindstx.org

SEPTEMBER

Sun	Mn	Tue	We	Thr	Fri	Sat
						1
2	3	4	5	6	7	8
9	10	11	12	13	14	15
16	17	18	19	20	21	22
23	24	25	26	27	28	29
30						

 # SEPTEMBER

SEP 15-16
Old Stone House Native American
Powwow & Cultural Festival
Intersection of Rt 8, Rt 173 & Rt 528
Slippery Rock
12 miles North of Butler PA
724 738 2408 David Dixon

SEP 15-16
Nause Waiwash Band of Indians Native
American Festival
Sailwinds Park
Cambridge MD
410 376 3889

SEP 19
San Jose Feast Day
Laguna Pueblo (Old Laguna) NM
505 843 7270

SEP 20-22
Elwah River Powwow
Longhouse Association
Location TBA
Port Angeles WA
360 457 4196 Linda Wiethman
360 457 9153 Doreen

SEP 21-22
Native American Celebration
Durham Technical Community College
1637 Lawson Street
Durham NC
919 686 3505

SEP 21-23
Native American Days
Angel Mounds State Historic Site
8215 Pollack Ave
Evansville IN 47715
812 853 3956 Bill Spellazza
812 479 5783 fax
curator@angelmounds.org

SEP 21-23
Northern Plains Tribal Arts Festival
Sioux Falls SD
800 658 4797

SEP 21-23
Baxoje Fall Encampment
Iowa Reservation
White Cloud KS
785 595 3306

SEP 21-23
Council Tree Powwow & Cultural
Festival
Confluence Park
Delta CO 81416
800 874 1741 Wilma or Glenna
970 874 8776 fax
counciltree@doci.net
www.counciltreepowwow.org

SEP 21-23
Middle Tennessee Powwow
Location: TBA
Lebanon TN
615 444 4899 Don Yahola

SEPTEMBER

SEP 21-23
Fall Equinox Festival
NC Indian Cultural Center
Pembroke, NC
910 521 4178

SEP 21-23
Blanchard Indian Powwow
Millstream Fairgrounds
Findlay OH
419 423-8194 Billy Nelson
bbrncody@aol.com

SEP 21-24
National Indian Days Celebration
White Swan WA
509 874 2473 Lindsey Selam

SEP 22-23
Indian Trail Powwow
Indian Trail Elementary School
Indian Trail NC

SEP 22-23
Ohio Shawnee Rendezvous
Zane Shawnee Caverns
St Rt 540
Bellefontain OH
937 592 9592
937 592 4458 fax
zaneshawneecaverns.org
704 535 4419

SEP 22-23 (Tentative)
Eschikagou Powwow Indian Trader's
Rendezvous
University of Chicago
Chicago IL
www.gatheringofnations.com

SEP 22-23
Indian Territory Arts and Humanities
Council (ITAHC) Original Doll Show and
Sale
Indian Territory Gallery
114 S. Main St.
Broken Arrow OK 74012
918 455 7347 DeLo Bookout
wbookout@busprod.com

SEPTEMBER

Sun	Mn	Tue	We	Thr	Fri	Sat
						1
2	3	4	5	6	7	8
9	10	11	12	13	14	15
16	17	18	19	20	21	22
23	24	25	26	27	28	29
30						

 # SEPTEMBER

SEP 22-23
Chickahominy Festival
8200 Lott Cary Road
Charles City Co VA
804 829 2186

SEP 25
St Elizabeth Feast Day
Laguna Pueblo (Paguate) NM
505 843 7270

SEP 29
San Geronimo Eve Vesper and Sundown
Dance
Taos Pueblo NM
505 843 7270

SEP 29-30
Eagle's Message Annual Powwow
Limestone County Sheriffs Arena
Hwy 99
Athens AL
256 729 1968 Marie Hill

SEP 29-30
Powwow By The Sea
Coastal Bend Council of Native
Americans
Memorial Coliseum
Corpus Christi TX
361 643 0399 Mari Lopez
tainalc@ccinternet.net

SEP 29-30
DeSoto Caverns Park Indian Fest
Childersburg AL
800 933 2283 Joe Beckham
256 378 3678
desoto@mindspring.com
www.cavern.com/desoto

SEP 29-30
Native American Foundation Powwow
Waimea Ballpark
Waimea HI
808 885 5569 Buttons Lovell

Last Weekend in SEP
Council of the Three Rivers American
Indian Center Annual Powwow
120 Charles Street
Dorseyville PA
412 782 4457

Last weekend in SEP
Northeastern Native American Assoc
Powwow
Roy Wilkens Park
Jamaica NY
718 978 7057

Last Weekend in SEP
Grand Bois Powwow
Grand Bois Park
Bourg LA
504 594 7410

SEP 30
San Geronimo Feast Day
Taos Pueblo NM
505 843 7270

SEP 30
Central Eastern Woodland Sokoki Tribe
of Algonquin Gathering
(Native People and members only)
13 Johnson
Rutland MA
508 886 8978

 # OCTOBER

SEP-OCT Dates TBA
Moving Waters Powwow
River Valley Resort
Canyon Lake TX
830 964 3613 John Guenzel/Sue Nelson
830 964 3620 fax
rioraft@gvtc.com
www.new-braunfels.com/rio/

OCT Date TBA
GLICA Harvest Festival
Greater Lowell Indian Cultural
Association
Pawtucket Indian Site
Tyngsboro MA
978 667 6498 evenings

OCT Date TBA
California Indian Storytelling Festival
Ohlone Community College
Fremont CA
510 794 7253 Lauren Teixeira
cistory@cistory.org
www.cistory.org

OCT Date TBA
Circle of Friends–Relatives of First
Americans Intertribal Powwow
Kapaa Beach Park
Kapaa, Kauai HI
808 335 8588

OCT Date TBA
Mat'Alyma Powwow
Nez Perce Reservation ID
208 935 2525

OCT Date TBA
American Indian Art Festival & Market
Annette Strauss Artist Square
Dallas TX
214 891 9640 Ms Pat Peterson
214 891 0221 fax
aiac@flash.net

OCT Date TBA
Cumberland County Native American
Association Powwow
Memorial Arena
Fayetteville NC
910 483 8442

OCT Date TBA
Indian Rodeo Finals
New Mexico State Fairgrounds
Albuquerque NM
505 488 6131
www.infrodeo.com

OCT Date TBA (near New Moon)
Eastern Kentucky Seventh Generation
Powwow
Old Time Machinery Grounds
Grayson KY
606 652 9850 Donna Church
606 652 4160 Christine Perkins

SEP 8-OCT 21
Lawrence Indian Arts Show
Haskell Indian Nations University
Lawrence KS
785 864 4245 Maria Martin
www.ukans.edu/~lias

 # OCTOBER

OCT 3-6
Moundville Native American Festival
Moundville Archaeological Park
Moundville AL
205 371 2234 Angie Jones
205 371 4180 fax
bbomar@bama.ua.edu (Bill Bomar)
moundvilee.ua.edu

OCT 4
San Francis de Assi Feast Day
Elk Dance
Nambe Pueblo NM
800 766 4405

OCT 5-7
Black Hills Powwow & Art Expo
Rushmore Plaza Civic Center
Rapid City SD
605 341 0925
art@rapidnet.com

OCT 6-7 & OCT 13-14
Spoon River Scenic Drive
17 Villages
Fulton County IL
309 647 8980 Karen Morse

OCT 6-7
Cal State San Marcos Traditional
Powwow
California State Univ—San Marcos
San Marcos CA
www.csusm.edu/powwow

OCT 6-7
American Indian Powwow Association
(AIPA) Intertribal Powwow
Thomas Square
Honolulu HI
808 734 5171 evening

OCT 6-7
Juried American Indian Arts Festival
Rankokus Indian Reservation
Rancocas NJ
609 261 4747
609 261 7313 fax
www.powhatan.org

OCT 6-31
Masters Art Show
Five Civilized Tribes Museum
Muskogee OK
918 683 1701 Clara Reekie
918 683 3070 fax
the5tribesmuseum@azalea.net
www.fivetribes.com

First Full Weekend in OCT
Damascus Powwow
Baseball Complex
Damascus VA
540 980 2203

First Weekend in OCT
1st Peoples Powwow
Gibralter Trade Crt
Mt Clements MI
810 756 1350
810 756 1352 fax
semii@mail.com

First Weekend in OCT
Council Oak Powwow
Rte 138
Dighton MA
508 880 6887

First Weekend in OCT
White Swan Indian Summer Celebration
Pavilion
White Swan WA
509 865 5121 Yakama Tourism
509 865 7570

First Weekend in OCT
Paucatuck Eastern Pequot Tribal Nation
Annual Harvest Moon Powwow
Highland Orchard Resort Park
North Stonington CT
860 448 0492

First Weekend in OCT
Five Nations Intertribal Powwow
Cherokee Nation of New Jersey
40th Street Park
Irvington NJ
973 374 1021 after 7 pm Chief C. W.
Longbow
973 375 3049 Ed Sunwolf

First Sunday in OCT
Mt Kearsarge Indian Museum Harvest
Moon Festival
Kearsarge Mt Rd
Warner NH
603 456 2600

OCT 7 (Tentative)
Native American Day Powwow
4-H Building
Vermillion SD
605 677 6875 Doyle
dtipeonh@usd.edu

Columbus Day Weekend (OCT 13-14)
Harvest Moon Festival & Powwow
Intertribal Council of Tolba Menahan
Lake Cochituate State Park
Nadick MA
978 546 8161

OCTOBER

Sun	Mn	Tue	We	Thr	Fri	Sat
	1	2	3	4	5	6
7	8	9	10	11	12	13
14	15	16	17	18	19	20
21	22	23	24	25	26	27
28	29	30	31			

 # OCTOBER

Columbus Day Weekend (OCT 13-14)
AIS Homecoming Powwow
Camp Marshall off Rte 31
Spencer MA
978 456 9707

Second Saturday in OCT
Muckleshoot Mini Powwow
Muckleshoot Tribal School
Auburn WA
253 939 3311 ext 153 Walter Pacheco
253 833 6177 fax

Second Saturday in OCT
Chaubunagungamaug Council
Harvestfest and Potluck
Nipmuck Reservation
School Street
Webster MA
413 436 5596

Second Weekend in OCT
American Indian Gathering
Community College of Beaver County
Monaca PA
724 775 8561, ext 157 Alex Gladis

Second Weekend in OCT
Honor the Earth Powwow
Lake Cochituate State Park
Nadick MA
978 546 8161

OCT 13-14
Hagerstown Powwow
Hagerstown Junior College
Hagerstown MD
252 257 5383

OCT 13-14 & OCT 6-7
Spoon River Scenic Drive
17 Villages
Fulton County IL
309 647 8980 Karen Morse

OCT 14
A Time of Thanksgiving
Lenni Lenape Historical Society
Museum of Indian Culture
Allentown PA
610 797 2121

OCT 17
St Margaret Mary Feast Day
Nambe Pueblo NM
505 843 7270

OCT 18-20
Indian Arts and Crafts Association Fall
Trade Show
Phoenix AZ
505 265 9149 Darien Cabral
505 474 8924 fax
IACA@IX.NETCOM.COM
www.IACA.com

OCT 19-21
Annual Powwow
Bending Water Park
Marion MD
410 623 2660
accohannock@crisfield.md
http://skipjack.net/le_shore/accohannock

Third Weekend in OCT
Waccamaw-Siouan Powwow
Buckhead near Bolton NC
910 655 8778 Priscilla Jacobs

Third Weekend in OCT
Native American Indian Fall Festival
Indian Plaza
Rte 2 Mohawk Trail
Charlemont MA
413 339 4096

Third Weekend in OCT
Native American Indian Association of
Tennessee Fall Festival and Powwow
Four Corners Water Park (Tentative)
Nashville TN
615 726 0806

Third Weekend in OCT
Ossahatchee Indian Festival
& Powwow
Soccer Complex
Hamilton GA
706 663 2313

Third Weekend in OCT
Land of Falling Waters Traditional
Powwow
Parkside Middle School
Jackson MI
517 768 8018 Heather Miller
616 781 6409 vendors Linda Cypret

Third Weekend in OCT
Wolf Den Powwow
Wolf Den State Park
Junction Rte 101 and 44
Pomfret Center CT
860 429 2668

OCT 21
UNACC Annual Fall Feast
Fort Devens
Ayer MA
978 772 1306

OCTOBER

Sun	Mn	Tue	We	Thr	Fri	Sat
1	2	3	4	5	6	
7	8	9	10	11	12	13
14	15	16	17	18	19	20
21	22	23	24	25	26	27
28	29	30	31			

 # OCTOBER

SEP 8-OCT 21
Lawrence Indian Arts Show
Haskell Indian Nations University
Lawrence KS
785 864 4245 Maria Martin
www.ukans.edu/~lias

OCT 26-27
Way South Powwow
Mc Allen TX
956 686 6696 Robert Soto
robtsoto@aol.com
956 583 1112 Betty Russell

OCT 26-28
Lumbee Fall Powwow
NC Indian Cultural Crt
Pembroke NC
910 521 8602

OCT 26-28
Southeastern Indian Intertribal Powwow
Chehaw Park
Albany GA
229 787 5180 Jerry Laney (evenings)
229 787 0642 fax
nativeway@mindspring.com
www.nativewayproductions.com

OCT 27
Apache Jii Day
Globe AZ
800 804 5623

OCT 27
Thunderbird American Indian Dancers
Powwow
American Indian Community House
404 Lafayette St
New York City NY
201 587 9633 Louis Mofsie

OCT 27
Valley of the Arkansas Powwow
Location TBA
Fort Smith AR
501 782 9099 Bob Titsworth
SBuch51371@aol.com

**OCT Weekend before Halloween
(OCT 27-28)**
Mid-Columbia River Annual Powwow
Celilo Indian Village
Celilo OR
509 865 5121 Yakama Tourism
509 865 7570 fax

OCT 28
Fires On The Frontier
SE Heritage Festival
Waleska GA
770 720 5971

THE POW WOW TRAIL

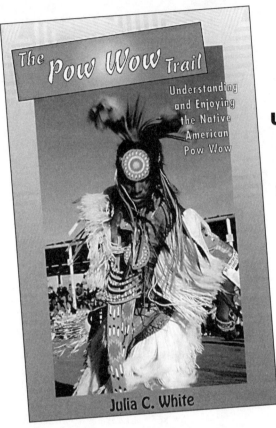

Understanding

and Enjoying

the Pow Wow

Julia C. White

The Pow Wow Trail is a guide to activities you might see at a pow wow. Each dance is described in detail, including background information and the history of the dance. Beautiful dynamic illustrations of pow wow dancers by Lenni-Lenape artist Diana Stanely convey the spirit of the event.

Book Publishing Company
P.O. Box 99
Summertown, TN 38483

1-800-695-2241

$8.95 US, $13.95 Canada
add $3 US or $3.50 Canada for shipping

NOVEMBER

NOV 3
NIU Gatherings
Northern Illinois University
De Kalb IL
815 753 0722 Rita
815 753 6366 fax
rreynolds@niu.edu

NOV 3-5
AIA Orlando Powwow
Central Florida Fairgrounds
Orlando FL
407 862 9676 Artie McRae

First Weekend in NOV
Trudeau Memorial Center Annual Indoor
Powwow
3445 Post Rd
Warwick RI
401 739 2992 Ed Egan

First Weekend in NOV
Stone Mountain Indian Festival &
National Powwow
Stone Mountain Park
Stone Mountain GA
770 735 6275

First Sunday in NOV
Dighton Council Oak Tree Ceremony &
Potluck
Old Town Hall Grange
Dighton MA
508 880 6887

NOV 9-11
American Indian Film Festival
3301 Lyon Street
San Francisco CA
415 554 0525
415 554 9542 fax
indianfilm@aifisf.com
www.aifisf.com

Second Saturday in NOV
Occoneechee Saponi Fall Festival
Powwow and Homecoming
Pleasant Grove Elementary School
Pleasant Grove NC
919 304 3723 Tribal Office
www.occaneechi-saponi.org/

Second Saturday in NOV
Muckleshoot Mini Powwow
Muckleshoot Tribal School
Auburn WA
253 939 3311 ext 153 Walter Pacheco
253 833 6177 fax

Second Weekend in NOV
American Indian Center of Chicago's
Contest Powwow Honoring Our
American Indian Center Community
University of Illinois
Chicago Pavilion 1150 W Harrison St
Chicago IL
773 275 5871 AIC
773 725 0319 fax
moperl@msn.com
AIC-www.mos.net/~aic
aic@aic-chicago.org
www.aic-chicago.org

Second Weekend in NOV
Mid American Native American
Southwestern & Western Fine Arts
Extravaganza
Convention Center
St Charles MO
561 465 2230 Dean & Jacie Davis

NOV 10-12
Yakama Nation Veterans Day Celebration
& Powwow
Pavilion
White Swan WA
509 865 5121 Yakama Tourism
509 865 7570 fax

NOV 10-12
Veterans Powwow
Duck Valley Reservation
Owyhee NV
775 757 3211

NOV 10-12
Veterans Memorial Powwow
San Carlos Apache Reservation
San Carlos AZ
520 475 3777 Dale Gilbert
520 475 2567 fax

NOV 12
San Diego Feast Day
Tesuque Pueblo NM
505 843 7270

NOV 14-17
Wild Game Festival
NC Indian Cultural Center
Pembroke NC
910 521 2433

NOV 16-18
Native Ways Indian Festival & Powwow
Georgia National Fairgrounds (I-75 exit
134)
Perry GA
229 787 5180 Jerry Laney (evenings)
229 787 0642 fax
nativeway@mindspring.com
www.NativeWayProductions.com

NOV 16-18
Noname Powwow
Jamil Shriner Temple, 208 Jamil Road
Columbia, SC
803 790 8214 Terence Little Water
4relations@angelfire.com
//fly to/AmericanIndianCenter

NOVEMBER

Sun	Mn	Tue	We	Thr	Fri	Sat
					1	2	3
4	5	6	7	8	9	10
11	12	13	14	15	16	17
18	19	20	21	22	23	24
25	26	27	28	29	30	

NOV 16-18
Great American Indian Expo
Richmond State Fairgrounds
Richmond VA
252 257 5383

NOV 17
Siletz Tribe's Restoration Celebration
Chinook Winds Gaming and Convention
Center
Lincoln City OR
800 922 1399 Craig Whitehead
541 444 2307 fax
craigw@ctsi.nsn.us

Weekend Before Thanksgiving
Bobby's Thanksgiving Festival
Bobby's Seminole Village
East Tampa, FL
813 620 3077

NOV 17-19
Young Nations Powwow
Nez Perce Tribe
Pi-Nee-Waus Community Building
Kamiah ID
208 276 7328 evenings

NOV 18-19
Indian Territory Fine Arts Festival
Broken Arrow Community Center
1500 S. Main St.
Broken Arrow OK 74012
918 259 1772 Bud
bud119320@netscape.net

Thanksgiving Weekend
Prairie Winds First Nations Powwow
Location TBA
Kansas City MO
913 768 4798

U.S. Thanksgiving Weekend
Canadian Aboriginal Festival
Toronto Skydome
Toronto ONT
519 751 0040
519 751 2790
canabfestival@home.com
www.canab.com

NOV 23-25
Indian Arts & Crafts Christmas Fair
California State Indian Museum
Sacramento CA
916 324 0971

NOV 24
Thunderbird American Indian Dancers
Auction
American Indian Community House
404 Lafayette St
New York City NY
201 587 9633 Louis Mofsie

DECEMBER

DEC All Month
Christmas Crafts Exhibit
Stewart Indian School Museum
Carson City NV
775 882 6929

First Weekend in DEC
Walatowa Winter Arts & Crafts
Jemez Pueblo NM
505 843 7270
505 834 7235

DEC 1-2
American Indian Art Show
Santa Clara Fairgrounds
San Jose CA
408 842 5977 Elizabeth
415 991 9181 Karen

DEC 2-3
North American Native Arts & Crafts
Festival
Vancouver Aboriginal Friendship Center
1607 East Hastings St
Vancouver BC CANADA
604 253 1020 Kat Norris
Kat@nativeworld.zzn.com

DEC 6
Christmas Parade of Lights/College
Christmas Bazaar
Navajo Community College
Tsaile AZ
520 724 6741

Second Weekend in DEC
Christmas Indian Market
Reno-Sparks Colony Gym
Reno NV
775 329 2936

Second Saturday in DEC
Muckleshoot Mini Powwow
Muckleshoot Tribal School
Auburn WA
253 939 3311 ext 153 Walter Pacheco
253 833 6177

Second Weekend in DEC
Annual Pueblo Grande Indian Market
South Mountain Park
Phoenix AZ
602 495 0901

DEC 12
Feast Day Mass
Dances after Mass
Pojoaque Pueblo NM
505 843 7270

DECEMBER

Sun	Mn	Tue	We	Thr	Fri	Sat
						1
2	3	4	5	6	7	8
9	10	11	12	13	14	15
16	17	18	19	20	21	22
23	24	25	26	27	28	29
30	31					

 # DECEMBER

DEC 15
Thunderbird American Indian Dancers
Powwow
American Indian Community House
404 Lafayette St
New York City NY
201 587 9633 Louis Mofsie

DEC 21-23
Winter Solstice Festival
NC Indian Cultural Center
Pembroke NC
910 521 4178

DEC 24-29
Christmas Celebrations and Dances:
Laguna Pueblo NM
Nambe Pueblo NM
Piruris Pueblo NM
San Felipe Pueblo NM
San Ildefonso Pueblo NM
San Juan Pueblo NM
Acoma Pueblo NM
Santa Ana Pueblo NM
Taos Pueblo NM
Tesuque Pueblo NM
Zia Pueblo NM
505 843 7270

DEC 25-28
Wapato Longhouse Christmas
Celebration & Powwow
Wapato Longhouse
Wapato WA
509 865 5121 Yakama Tourism
509 865 7570 fax

DEC 28-31
Paxam SIS New Year's Powwow
Nespelem Community Center
Nespelem WA
509 634 4711
509 634 2110 Shelly Davis

DEC 29-JAN 1
Toppenish Creek New Years Celebration
Toppenish Creek Longhouse
White Swan WA
509 865 5121 ext. 408
509 865 7570 fax

DEC 30-31
Tipton Mid-Winter Powwow
Tipton County Fairgrounds
4-H Building
Tipton IN
317 773 4233 Barbara Scott
jasco@iquest.net
317 745 2858 Ray Kappmeyer, after 6 PM
http://tlodge.srphoto.net

DEC 30-JAN 1
New Year Powwow
Nespelem WA
509 634 4711

DEC 30-JAN 1
In the Spirit of the New Year
Community Center
Naytahwaush MN
218 846 9749 days
218 573 2190

DEC 31-JAN 1
Leech Lake New Years Powwow
Old Cass Lake High School
Leech Lake MN
218 335 8289

DEC 31-JAN 1
Mid-Winter Powwow
New Town ND
701 759 3469
701 627 3642

DEC 31-JAN 3
Lodge Grass New Years Celebration
Lodge Grass MT
406 638 2601

Powwow Activity Book

Sandy & Jesse T. Hummingbird

A delightful activities book for children ages five to ten years old. Using imagery of the Native American powwow and its dancers, Sandy and Jesse have created enjoyable lessons in matching, mazes, completing sentences, crossword puzzles, connecting dots, counting, coloring, spelling, and more.

$4.95
Please include $3.00 per
book shipping

Book Publishing Company
P.O. Box 99
Summertown, TN 38483
1-800-695-2241

 **LOCATION LISTINGS**

In this section events are listed by state or province. Additional information is on the page indicated after each event.

CANADA

Canada's National Aboriginal Day—Community Events Across Canada: www.aboriginalday.com

 **LOCATION LISTINGS**

UNITED KINGDOM

For information on all U. K. powwows please contact:
John Hamling
The World of the North American Indian
51 Rushdean Road
Rochester, Kent
ME2 2PA, England

011 44 1634 318518

or email at fullcircle@written.freeserve.co.uk

 **LOCATION LISTINGS**

UNITED STATES

 **LOCATION LISTINGS**

 **LOCATION LISTINGS**

Michigan

 **LOCATION LISTINGS**

New York

 **LOCATION LISTINGS**

 **LOCATION LISTINGS**

Wisconsin

ORDER NOW

POWWOW CALENDAR 2002

Available December 2001

The definitive guide to
Native American:
  ° Powwows
  ° Dances
  ° Craft Fairs
  ° Cultural Events

Each entry includes :
  ° Date
  ° Event
  ° Location
  ° Phone Number

BOOK PUBLISHING COMPANY
PO BOX 99
SUMMERTOWN, TN 38483
for MasterCard and Visa orders,
call 1-800-695-2241

Please send me ____ copy (s) of the *2002 Powwow Calendar*

Name _____

Address _____

City, Street, Zip _____

Enclose check or money order for $12.95 per book ($9.95 + $3.00 shipping). Canadian orders: Enclose a Canadian postal union money order for $13.95 US ($9.95 + $3.50 shipping).

Send to Book Publishing Co., PO Box 99, Summertown, TN 38483

MAR 31
California State University Powwow
Uniting Our People
Stanislaus
209 667 3598 Mami
MALLgire@stan.csustan.edu

APR Date TBA
Apigsigtag Ta Reconciliation Powwow
Native American Cultural Center
University of New Hampshire
Location TBA
Durham NH
603 862 0231

APR 14
Spring Intertribal Social & Powwow
Civic Center
268 Gallison Hill Road
Montpelier VT
802 229 0601 Patty Maning

APR 16-22
Arizona State University American Indian
Culture Week
Tempe AZ
480 965 8044

APR 18-19
Dawnland Country Summer Red Road
Parker's Field
E. Montpelier VT
802 229 0601 Patty Maning
888 211 1840

APR 20-22
Arizona State University Spring
Competition Powwow
Tempe AZ
480 965 5224
http://powwow.asu.edu

JUN 22-24
White Buffalo Gazette Intertribal
Powwow
Sedgwick County Park
Wichita KS
316 524 1210 Mike or Susan Seal
Chocbuff@worldnet.att.net

JUL 21-22
Native American Iroquois Veterans
Association (NAIVA)
Annual Powwow
Veterans Park
Salamanca NY
716 283 0084

OCT 20
Texas Lumbee Tribe Powwow
Roberston County Fairgrounds
Hearne TX
979 828 4977 Chief Alleen Fallen Leaf
Perkins